CHINESE
WITHOUT TEARS
—
ADVANCED

Discovery Publisher

©2017, Discovery Publisher
All rights reserved

No part of this book may be reproduced in any form or by any electronic or mechanical means including information storage and retrieval systems, without permission in writing from the publisher.

Author : Liu Huijun
Translation: Jared Scott Pratt

616 Corporate Way, Suite 2-4933
Valley Cottage, New York, 10989
www.discoverypublisher.com
edition@discoverypublisher.com
facebook.com/discoverypublisher
twitter.com/discoverypb

New York • Paris • Dublin • Tokyo • Hong Kong

AN ENGLISH FOREWORD FOR LEARNERS

This textbook includes 16 lessons, each centering on a conversational scenario likely to be encountered by anyone living in, studying in, or visiting China for the first time. Each lesson focuses on a single topic, such as asking and giving directions, changing currencies, using public transportation, ordering in restaurants, discussing the weather, renting an apartment, and asking for help with repairs.

The dialogues presented in each lesson are accompanied by detailed notes on grammar and usage, supplementary information, and exercises. Together, they follow the story of an overseas student, Emily, through the course of her time in China, each lesson building on the one preceding it to provide increasingly sophisticated conversations and increasingly complex language instruction.

The Chinese text was compiled within Shenzhen University's College of International Exchange by associate professor Liu Huijun. The English translation was written by a native speaker from the United States in collaboration with Professor Liu.

This textbook is the third volume of the *Chinese Without Tears* series. It is recommended for intermediate beginners, either those who have studied *Chinese Without Tears for Beginners* and *Chinese Without Tears, Intermediate Level* or with two semester's study in Mandarin Chinese program or those with equivalent experience (in part-time courses or through self-study). Both a thorough knowledge of Pinyin (拼音) and a rudimentary knowledge of Hanzi (汉字) are recommended for learners studying this textbook.

Lessons are divided into the following sections:

1. A text of the lesson's dialogue, in both Chinese and English, is accompanied by a video recording. All dialogues include the real-life, up-to-date language used in daily life, language that learners can hear and use every day.
2. A series of comprehension questions aids learners in determining whether they understand all of the important parts of the dialogue
3. A list of vocabulary shows new words first in their smallest meaningful parts, then as presented in the dialogues. New vocabulary items number 900 over all 16 lessons.
4. Word Usage sections explain the target vocabulary's grammatical and colloquial usage in detail and illustrate ideas with sample sentences (including commonly made errors). In addition, "Distinguish" sections in many lessons focus on words and structures with easily confused meanings, uses, or connotations and highlight differences with detailed explanations and multiple examples.
5. Chinese Knowledge sections provide additional insight into the formation and grammar of the language.
6. Cultural Tips and Tips for Daily Life provide information on customs and common problems in mainland China, helping learners avoid common problems while getting the most out of living in China.
7. Supplementary Terms and Supplementary Information sections provide learners with the words and knowledge they need to discuss topics in greater depth.
8. A variety of exercises reinforces the vocabulary and grammar covered in each lesson. Discussion, performance and role-playing activities give level-appropriate speaking and interaction opportunities to those studying in classroom settings or with friends or co-workers.

The 16 lessons together present a full course of spoken Chinese for beginners. In a classroom setting, each lesson should require approximately 4-6 class hours. The lessons are arranged in order of increasing difficulty. Successful study of all 16 lessons should prepare most learners for study at an *intermediate* level.

Notes on the English translation: the translation of this text into English follows two simple principles:

1. For the dialogues, the English translation closely follows the original Chinese text. Whenever it was possible to do so without interfering with meaning, the original language's word order and choices have been closely reflected in the English version. It is hoped this will make remembering the dialogues easier for learners.
2. In all other sections, translations have been kept as clear and simple as possible, avoiding specialized linguistic and grammatical terms except where unavoidable. The Chinese characters discussed in each note are left intact in order to avoid potential confusion between English and Chinese usage.

目录

TABLE OF CONTENTS

AN ENGLISH FOREWORD FOR LEARNERS I

TABLE OF CONTENTS II

LESSON 1: HOW IS THE WEATHER GOING TO BE TOMORROW IN SHENZHEN? 1

- 一 • Text 1
- 二 • Answer the following questions according to the text 2
- 三 • Vocabulary 3
- 四 • Word Usage 4
- 五 • Chinese Knowledge 6
- 六 • Related Terms: weather 7
- 七 • Tips for Daily Life: weather advisory 7
- 八 • Exercises 8

LESSON 2: YOUR HOME IS REALLY BEAUTIFUL! 13

- 一 • Text 13
- 二 • Answer the following questions according to the text 15
- 三 • Vocabulary 15
- 四 • Word Usage 16
- 五 • Chinese Knowledge 18
- 六 • Related Terms: hobbies 18
- 七 • Cultural Tips: common phrases & Tieguanyin tea 19
- 八 • Exercises 19

LESSON 3: YOU WANT TO RENT AN APARTMENT? 23

- 一 • Text 23
- 二 • Answer the following questions according to the text 25

三 • Vocabulary	26
四 • Word Usage	27
五 • Chinese Knowledge	29
六 • Related Terms: rentals	29
七 • Tips for Daily Life: dormitory & ADSL	29
八 • Exercises	30

LESSON 4: CAN YOU SELL IT ANY CHEAPER? — 33

一 • Text	33
二 • Answer the following questions according to the text	35
三 • Vocabulary	35
四 • Word Usage	36
五 • Chinese Knowledge	39
六 • Related Terms: prices	39
七 • Cultural Links: Shenzhen shopping areas	39
八 • Exercises	40

LESSON 5: MY ROOM'S FAUCET IS BROKEN — 43

一 • Text	43
二 • Answer the following questions according to the text	45
三 • Vocabulary	46
四 • Word Usage	46
五 • Chinese Knowledge	48
六 • Related Terms: household items & problems	49
七 • Cultural Tips: receipts & use of "马上"	49
八 • Exercises	50

LESSON 6: WHAT NEW HAIRSTYLE DO YOU WANT? — 53

一 • Text	53
二 • Answer the following questions according to the text	55
三 • Vocabulary	55
四 • Word Usage	56
五 • Chinese Knowledge	59
六 • Related Terms: beauty salons	60

| 七 | • | Tips for Daily Life: "洗头" | 60 |
| 八 | • | Exercises | 60 |

LESSON 7: WE CAN GO LISTEN TO A CONCERT, OK? — 63

一	•	Text	63
二	•	Answer the following questions according to the text	65
三	•	Vocabulary	65
四	•	Word Usage	66
五	•	Chinese Knowledge	68
六	•	Related Terms: entertainment	69
七	•	Cultural Tips: China festivals & dating	69
八	•	Exercises	70

LESSON 8: WHICH KIND OF MEDICINE WORKS FAST? — 73

一	•	Text	73
二	•	Answer the following questions according to the text	75
三	•	Vocabulary	76
四	•	Word Usage	77
五	•	Chinese Knowledge	77
六	•	Related Terms: illness	78
七	•	Tips for Daily Life: emergency numbers	78
八	•	Exercises	78

LESSON 9: I LIKE THE GIANT PANDAS THE MOST — 81

一	•	Text	81
二	•	Answer the following questions according to the text	83
三	•	Vocabulary	83
四	•	Word Usage	84
五	•	Chinese Knowledge	86
六	•	Related Terms: animals and plants	86
七	•	Cultural Tips: Shenzhen parks	87
八	•	Exercises	87

LESSON 10: WE'LL GO OUT TOGETHER AND CELEBRATE, OK?   91

- 一 • Text   91
- 二 • Answer the following questions according to the text   93
- 三 • Vocabulary   94
- 四 • Word Usage   96
- 五 • Chinese Knowledge   98
- 六 • Related terms and information   99
- 七 • Tips for Daily Life: Shenzhen KTVs   100
- 八 • Exercises   100

LESSON 11: WHAT SORT OF CITY IS SHENZHEN?   103

- 一 • Text   103
- 二 • Answer the following questions according to the text   105
- 三 • Vocabulary   105
- 四 • Word Usage   107
- 五 • Chinese Knowledge   108
- 六 • Related Terms: the Internet   109
- 七 • Cultural Tips: Shenzhen introduction   109
- 八 • Exercises   110

LESSON 12: YOUR TRIP HERE WAS STRENUOUS!   113

- 一 • Text   113
- 二 • Answer the following questions according to the text   115
- 三 • Vocabulary   116
- 四 • Word Usage   117
- 五 • Chinese Knowledge   121
- 六 • Commonly used polite expressions   121
- 七 • Cultural Tips: more polite expressions   122
- 八 • Exercises   122

LESSON 13: I WANT TO FIND WORK IN SHENZHEN   125

- 一 • Text   125
- 二 • Answer the following questions according to the text   127
- 三 • Vocabulary   127

四	•	WORD USAGE	**128**
五	•	CHINESE KNOWLEDGE	**129**
六	•	RELATED TERMS: EMPLOYMENT	**129**
七	•	TIPS FOR DAILY LIFE: SHENZHEN JOBS	**131**
八	•	EXERCISES	**131**

LESSON 14: WHAT PRESENTS ARE GOOD TO TAKE BACK TO MY COUNTRY? **133**

一	•	TEXT	**133**
二	•	ANSWER THE FOLLOWING QUESTIONS ACCORDING TO THE TEXT	**134**
三	•	VOCABULARY	**135**
四	•	WORD USAGE	**136**
五	•	CHINESE KNOWLEDGE	**138**
六	•	RELATED TERMS: POPULAR CHINESE PRESENTS FOR FOREIGNERS	**138**
七	•	CULTURAL TIPS: ARTS & TABOOS	**139**
八	•	EXERCISES	**140**

LESSON 15: PLACES WORTH VISITING IN CHINA ARE TOO MANY TO LIST **143**

一	•	TEXT	**143**
二	•	ANSWER THE FOLLOWING QUESTIONS ACCORDING TO THE TEXT	**145**
三	•	VOCABULARY	**145**
四	•	WORD USAGE	**146**
五	•	CHINESE KNOWLEDGE	**148**
六	•	RELATED TERMS: CHINA'S FAMOUS SCENIC AND HISTORICAL SITES	**148**
七	•	CULTURAL TIPS: TRAVEL WEBSITES	**149**
八	•	EXERCISES	**150**

LESSON 16: MAY FAVORABLE WINDS SPEED YOU ON YOUR WAY! **153**

一	•	TEXT	**153**
二	•	ANSWER THE FOLLOWING QUESTIONS ACCORDING TO THE TEXT	**155**
三	•	VOCABULARY	**155**
四	•	WORD USAGE	**156**
五	•	CHINESE KNOWLEDGE	**157**
六	•	RELATED TERMS: CONGRATULATIONS	**158**

七 • CULTURAL TIPS: MAJOR FESTIVALS IN CHINA	**158**
八 • EXERCISES	**158**

ANSWERS TO EXERCISES **161**

INDEX OF VOCABULARY WORDS **173**

第一课 / LESSON 1

明天深圳天气怎么样?
HOW IS THE WEATHER GOING TO BE TOMORROW IN SHENZHEN?

这一课我们将学到 • In this lesson we will study the following:
1. 与天气有关的内容
2. 重点词语:越来越……、明天比今天还热吗?、你看这天气……、还行
3. 汉语知识:汉语中的"比字句"

一、课文 • Text

(吴帅和艾美丽在谈论中国的气候 • Wu Shuai and Emily are discussing China's climate)

艾美丽: 这里的夏天太热了!中国的夏天都很热吗?
Here, summer is too hot. Are the summers here all really hot?

吴帅: 是的,大部分地区都很热,而且常常下雨。
They are. Most places are all really hot. Also, it often rains.

艾美丽: 美国的夏天经常刮飓风,这里会吗?
In the United States during summer, we frequently have hurricanes. Does that happen here?

吴帅: 中国的南方也经常刮风,但是我们不叫"飓风",我们叫"台风"。
China's southern areas also frequently have strong windstorms, but we don't call them "hurricanes." We call them "typhoons" (táifēng).

艾美丽: 中国的冬天会下雪吗?
In China, during winter, does it snow?

吴帅: 南方的冬天很少下雪,深圳的冬天从不下雪。不过,北方的冬天常常下雪。在冬天,北方比南方冷多了。哈尔滨的冬天最低气温有零下四十度呢。
In southern areas, during winter we rarely have snow. In Shenzhen, it never snows. However, in the northern areas, during winter there is often snow. In winter, the North gets much colder than the South. In Ha'erbin, during winter, the lowest temperatures are -40°C.

艾美丽: 那春天和秋天呢？怎么样？
Then, spring and autumn? What about them?

吴帅: 春天和秋天不冷也不热，挺舒服的。不过，春天有点儿潮湿，秋天比较干燥。
Spring and autumn are not cold and not hot. They're very comfortable. Spring is a little humid. Autumn is comparatively dry.

艾美丽: 你看了今天的天气预报吗？明天深圳天气怎么样？
Did you see today's weather forecast? How is the weather going to be tomorrow in Shenzhen?

吴帅: 看了，明天早上是晴天，下午是阴天，傍晚有阵雨，风不大。
I saw it. Tomorrow morning will be sunny. The afternoon will be overcast. The evening will have a bit of rain. The wind won't be strong.

艾美丽: 明天比今天还热吗？
Will tomorrow be even hotter than today?

吴帅: 是啊，明天的气温比今天高三度。夏天到了，天气越来越热了。
It will. Tomorrow's temperature will be 3°C higher than today's. Once summer arrives, the weather becomes hotter and hotter.

艾美丽: 我明天想去野餐，你看这天气合适吗？
Tomorrow I want to go to on a picnic. Do you think the weather will be suitable?

吴帅: 还行吧。别忘了擦防晒霜，也要带上雨伞。
It should still be OK. Don't forget to apply sunscreen. Also, you should carry an umbrella.

艾美丽: 好的，谢谢你。
OK, thank you.

二、根据课文回答问题 · ANSWER THE FOLLOWING QUESTIONS ACCORDING TO THE TEXT

1. 中国的夏天都很热吗？

2. 深圳的冬天下雪吗？

3. 台风在什么地方刮？

4. 中国大部分的地方春天和秋天怎么样？

5. 艾美丽想去野餐，吴帅跟他说了什么？

三、生词 • Vocabulary

1	明天	míngtiān	名	tomorrow
2	天气	tiānqì	名	weather
3	谈论	tánlùn	动	to discuss, to talk about
4	气候	qìhòu	名	climate
5	夏天	xiàtiān	名	summer
6	热	rè	形	hot (high in temperature)
7	部分	bùfen	名	part, percentage
8	地区	dìqū	名	area
9	而且	érqiě	连	also, in addition
10	常常	chángchang	副	often, always
11	下（雨）	xià (yǔ)	动	(of rain or snow) to fall, to have
12	雨	yǔ	名	rain
13	下雨	xià//yǔ	（动宾）动	to rain
14	刮	guā	动	blow (of strong winds)
15	飓风	jùfēng	名	hurricane
16	南方	nánfāng	名	southern regions, the South
17	风	fēng	名	wind
18	台风	táifēng	名	typhoon
19	冬天	dōngtiān	名	winter
20	雪	xuě	名	snow
21	少	shǎo	形	rarely, seldom
22	从不	cóngbù		never
23	北方	běifāng	名	northern regions, the North
24	比	bǐ	介	compare(d) to, than
25	低	dī	形	low
26	气温	qìwēn	名	temperature
27	零下	língxià	名	subzero, below zero
28	度	dù	量	[a measure word, degree]
29	春天	chūntiān	名	spring
30	秋天	qiūtiān	名	autumn
31	舒服	shūfu	形	comfortable
32	潮湿	cháoshī	形	humid
33	干燥	gānzào	形	dry, not humid
34	预报	yùbào	动、名	to forecast; forecast
35	早上	zǎoshang	名	morning
36	晴	qíng	形	(of weather) sunny

37	阴	yīn	形	(of weather) overcast
38	傍晚	bàngwǎn	名	nightfall, dusk, evening
39	阵	zhèn	量	[measure word indicating brief periods of rain]
40	阵雨	zhènyǔ		rain shower
41	高	gāo	形	high, tall
42	越来越……	yuèláiyuè……		more and more…
43	野餐	yěcān	名	picnic
44	擦	cā	动	rub, wipe, apply
45	防	fáng	动	to prevent, to protect against
46	晒	shài	动	(of the sun) to shine
47	霜	shuāng	名	frost; white
48	防晒霜	fángshàishuāng	名	sunscreen
49	雨伞	yǔsǎn		umbrella

专名词 • Proper Names

| 50 | 美国 | měiguó | | United States of America |
| 51 | 哈尔滨 | hāěrbīn | | Ha'erbin (Harbin) |

四、词语解释 • Word Usage

（一）、越来越……

汉语中，"越来越……"表示随着时间的变化，情况的状态、程度发生变化。"越来越"后面通常接形容词，而不能接副词。

越来越 indicates a change in conditions or of degree over time. It is most often followed by an adjective. It may not be followed by adverbs such as 很, 太, or 非常.

例如： 1. 五月以后天气越来越热了。
　　　 2. 最近他的病越来越严重。
　　　 3. 他的汉语越来越很好。（×）

我们来造句 • Make your own sentence

（二）、明天比今天还热吗？

"还"在这里是"更"、"更加"的意思，也可以用"更"表示。常用在比较句中，表示比较程度的差别。在 "A比B还高" 的句子中，意思是：B已经比一般的程度高，或是达到某种程度，A则比B的程度高。

Here, 还 has the same meaning as 更 or 更加. It is often used when making comparisons to emphasize a difference in degree. For example, in the sentence "A 比 B 还高," the meaning is that B is already quite tall and that A is taller still. 更 can be used instead of 还 in such sentences.

例如： 1. 我的汉语好，他比我的汉语还好。
2. 英语难，汉语比英语还难。
3. 我比他更像妈妈。
4. 他今天比我来得还早。

我们来造句 • Make your own sentence

（三）、你**看**这天气合适吗？

在这里，"看"的意思是"觉得"、"认为"的意思。常用来表达主观的看法。后面不能带宾语，而只能接小句或短语。

Here, 看 means to think or to consider. It is often used when expressing personal opinions. When used in this way, 看 must be followed by a complete clause.

例如： 1. 你看我穿这条裙子还好看吗？
2. 你看这么做可以吗？
3. 我看你不适合做这件事。

我们来造句 • Make your own sentence

（四）、**还行吧**

在这里，"还"表达程度低或勉强、谦虚的语气，"还行"的意思是还可以，不到好的程度。常用的形式有"还好"、"还不错"、"还可以"、"还行"等。在与一般的形容词连用时，常在形容词前加上"算"。比如"还算便宜"、"还算凉快"、"还算漂亮" 等等。

Here, 还 indicates a low but acceptable degree. 还行 indicates that the situation is less than desirable but still acceptable. 还好, 还不错, and 还可以 are all common expressions with similar meanings. The expression 还算 (roughly meaning "can be considered") is also common, as in 还算便宜, 还算凉快, 还算漂亮, and others.

例如： 1. A：你的汉语怎么样？
B：还可以。
2. A：这个菜好吃吗？
B：还行。
3. 这件衣服还算便宜，你买吧。

我们来造句 • Make your own sentence

五、汉语知识 • Chinese Knowledge

语中的"比字句" • Sentence patterns using 比

汉语中常用"比"字表达比较的意思,主要形式有:

比 is often used in sentences to make comparisons. Important uses include the following:

▶ (一)、比字词组+形容词

The pattern "A+比+B+adj" states a difference in degree between A and B.

例如: 1. 他比我高。

2. 他比我跑得快。

3. 他汉语说得比我好。

▶ (二)、比字词组+形容词+"得多/多了"(表示比较的程度)

The pattern "A+比+B+adj+得多/多了" emphasizes a large difference between A and B.

例如: 1. 他的房间比我的大得多。

2. 他的房间比我的大多了。

<u>注意</u>:(1)在这种句子中,不能将程度副词"很"、"最"、"非常"放在形容词前表示程度,而是在形容词后加"多"、"远"等词来表示。

Note: (1) In this sentence pattern, most adverbs of degree, such as 很, 最, and 非常, cannot be used. Instead 多 or 远 should be used after the adjective.

例如: 1. 我的汉语比他很差。 (×)

2. 我的汉语比他差得远了。 (√)

3. 我的汉语比他差得多。 (√)

4. 他的房间比我的非常小。 (×)

5. 他的房间比我的小得多。 (√)

<u>注意</u>:(2)在这种句子中,可以在形容词前加上"还"和"更"等程度副词,表示比较程度的差别。

Note: (2) In this sentence pattern, 还 or 更 can be placed before the adjective to add emphasis.

例如: 1. 他的汉语比我的还好。

2. 她的衣服比我的更多。

▶ (三)、比字词组+形容词+数量词组

The pattern "A+比+B+adj+number+measure word" shows a difference in quantity.

例如: 1. 他比我大两岁。

2. 他的房间比我的大两平方米。

<u>注意</u>:这种句子中,数量词组要放在形容词后,补充说明数量,不能放在形容词前。

Note: The number and measure word are placed after, not before, the adjective.

六、相关链接，常用的有关天气的词语 • Related Terms: weather

1	晴间多云	qíngjiànduōyún	partly cloudy
2	多云	duōyún	cloudy
3	阴天	yīntiān	overcast
4	阴间多云	yīnjiànduōyún	mostly cloudy
5	雷阵雨	léizhènyǔ	thunder storm
6	小雨	xiǎoyǔ	sprinkle (light rain)
7	中雨	zhōngyǔ	moderate rain
8	大雨	dàyǔ	heavy rainfall
9	暴雨	bàoyǔ	rainstorm; thunderstorm
10	小雪	xiǎoxuě	light snow
11	中雪	zhōng xuě	moderate snow
12	大雪	dàxuě	heavy snow
13	暴雪	bàoxuě	blizzard

七、文化生活小贴士 • Tips for Daily Life: weather advisory

（一）、深圳市气象局官方网站

Meteorological Bureau of Shenzhen Municipality homepage: szmb.gov.cn

（二）、常见天气预警图标 • Common weather advisory symbols

▶ **暴雨 • Rainstorm**

黄色暴雨信号：6小时内可能或者已经受暴雨影响。
Amber rainstorm signal: Storms have occurred or are likely within a six-hour period.

橙色暴雨信号：3小时内可能或者已经受暴雨影响，降雨量50毫米以上。
Orange rainstorm signal: Storms have occurred or are likely within a three-hour period. Rainfall may exceed 50mm.

红色暴雨信号：3小时内可能或者已经受暴雨影响，降雨量100毫米以上。（幼儿园、托儿所和中小学停课）
Red rainstorm signal: Storms have occurred or are likely within a three-hour period. Rainfall may exceed 100mm. (Nursery schools, primary schools and middle schools suspend classes.)

▶ **台风 • Typhoon**

白色风球：48小时内可能受热带气旋影响。
White typhoon signal: Tropical storms are likely within a 48-hour period.

蓝色风球：24小时内可能或者已经受热带气旋影响，平均风力6级以上。
Blue typhoon signal: Tropical storms rated 6 or higher on the Beaufort scale are likely within a 24-hour period.

黄色风球：24小时内可能或者已经受热带气旋影响,平均风力8级以上。(幼儿园、托儿所和中小学停课,停止高空、水上等户外作业,船舶到避风场所避风；危险地带人员撤离,停止露天集体活动,立即疏散人员)
Yellow typhoon signal: Tropical storms rated 8 or higher on the Beaufort scale are likely within a 24-hour period. (Nursery schools, primary schools and middle schools suspend classes. Flights and aquatic activities are suspended. Sea-going vessels take harbor. Evacuations are conducted and open-air activities are cancelled.)

橙色风球：12小时内可能或者已经受热带气旋影响,平均风力10级以上。
Orange typhoon signal: Tropical storms rated 10 or higher on the Beaufort scale are likely within a 12-hour period.

红色风球：6小时内可能或者已经受热带气旋影响,平均风力12级以上。(建议全市停业)
Red typhoon signal: Tropical storms rated 12 or higher on the Beaufort scale are likely within a 6-hour period. (All businesses close city-wide.)

▶ **高温** · **High temperatures**

黄色高温信号：24小时内可能或者已经受暖空气影响,最高气温升至35℃以上。(避免长时间户外或者高温条件下的作业)
Yellow high-temperature signal: Temperatures up to 35° C are expected within a 24-hour period. (Longtime exposure to direct sunlight should be avoided.)

橙色高温信号：24小时内可能或者已经受暖空气影响,最高气温升至37℃以上。(建议12－15时停止户外或者高温条件下作业,并缩短连续作业时间)
Orange high-temperature signal: Temperatures up to 37° C are expected within a 24-hour period. (Outdoor work should be suspended from 12 o'clock to 15 o'clock or limited to brief time periods.)

红色高温信号：24小时内可能或者已经受暖空气影响,最高气温升至40℃以上。(建议停止户外或者高温条件下作业)
Red high-temperature signal: Temperatures up to 40° C are expected in a 24-hour period. (Longtime exposure to direct sunlight should be avoided.)

八、练习 · Exercises

（一）、填上合适的词语 · Fill in the blanks with appropriate words

谈论＿＿＿、＿＿＿　　　　从不＿＿＿、＿＿＿
天气＿＿＿、＿＿＿　　　　部分＿＿＿、＿＿＿
刮＿＿＿　下＿＿＿　　　　东＿＿＿西＿＿＿
上＿＿＿　左＿＿＿　　　　春＿＿＿秋＿＿＿

（二）、选词填空 · Fill in the blanks with the words provided

谈论　气候　地区　从不　零下　舒服　干燥　野餐

1. 已经冬天了,北方很多地方都是＿＿＿＿＿十几度。
2. 他们常常在一起＿＿＿＿＿中国文化。
3. 吴帅以前＿＿＿＿＿喝酒,今天是第一次。
4. 如果你觉得不＿＿＿＿＿,就先回去吧。

5. 深圳的_____跟我们国家不一样，我不太习惯。
6. 我们本来打算去_____，因为下雨就没去。
7. 天气_____应该少吃辣椒。
8. 中国的大部分_____夏天都很热。

（三）、用所给的词语完成句子 • Answer the questions using the words in parentheses

1. A：你喜欢一个人喝酒吗？
   B：_____。（从不）
2. A：深圳夏天的天气怎么样？
   B：_____。（而且）
3. A：王老师的课你能听得懂吗？
   B：_____。（部分）
4. A：你多长时间给妈妈打一次电话？
   B：_____。（常常）
5. A：你现在习惯吃中国菜了吗？
   B：_____。（越来越）
6. A：你觉得今天会下雨吗？
   B：_____。（看）

（四）、说明下面句中"上"的意思或用法

Explain the meaning of 上 in the following sentences

1. 今天吴帅请我吃饭，有一道菜的名字叫"蚂蚁<u>上</u>树"。
2. 请<u>上</u>二楼交费。
3. 大家都到了，请服务员<u>上</u>菜吧。
4. 我觉得有点儿冷，把空调关<u>上</u>吧。
5. 菜单<u>上</u>面有很多菜，我看不懂。
6. 公交车<u>上</u>有很多人。
7. 我要去<u>上</u>课了。
8. 早<u>上</u>好！

（五）、写出反义词 • Write an antonym for each of the following words

大___	对___	买___	上___	肥___
冷___	高___	潮湿___	多___	快___
阴___	左___	开___	前___	黑___

（六）、模仿例句，用"比"字句改写这些句子

Following the example, rewrite each sentence using the 比 sentence patterns.

例句：今天气温25度，昨天气温30度。
　　　今天气温**比**昨天低。昨天气温**比**今天高。

1. 小王180cm，小张175cm。
   _____

2. 坐出租车15分钟，坐公交车50分钟。
   _____

3. 我会写200个汉字，他会写180个汉字。
   _____

4. 啤酒5块钱一瓶，饮料3块钱一瓶。
   _____

5. 从学校到我家800米远，从银行到我家200米远。
   _____

6. 老师28岁，学生18岁。
   _____

（七）、我是天气预报员 • Role-Play: Meteorologist

看下面的天气图，为大家作一个简短的天气预报，内容包括：地名、天气情况、最高气温、最低气温

Perform a brief weather report based on the following graphics. Include names of cities, weather conditions, and high and low temperatures.

（以下资料来自天气在线网 t7online.com，2011年3月28日的天气）

The following was downloaded from t7online.com on 2011/03/28.

| 晴 | 晴间多云 | 多云 |
| 阴 | 多云，有阵雨 | 小雪 |

阴到多云，有雪

香港 地区天气预报			
文字版	3月28日	3月29日	3月30日
最低温度	14°C	17°C	18°C
最高温度	22°C	25°C	21°C
上午	☀️	☀️	☁️
下午	☀️	☀️	☁️
晚上	🌙	🌧️	🌧️

东京 地区天气预报			
文字版	3月28日	3月29日	3月30日
最低温度	4°C	5°C	6°C
最高温度	12°C	15°C	15°C
上午	☀️	☀️	☀️
下午	☀️	☀️	☀️
晚上	🌙	🌙	🌙

马尼拉 地区天气预报			
文字版	3月28日	3月29日	3月30日
最低温度	25°C	24°C	25°C
最高温度	31°C	32°C	30°C
上午	🌧️	☁️	☁️
下午	🌧️	☁️	☁️
晚上	🌧️	🌧️	🌧️

（八）、在老师的帮助下写出常用的天气信号图标的含义

With your teacher's help, label the following charts

（九）、趣味播报 • Humorous Broadcast

Prepare an entertaining weather report to present to the class, as below:

比如：11月21日中午到傍晚，多云，有短时冰淇淋雨，记得带杯子来接冰淇淋；巧克力风2-3级；沿海的巧克力风风力4级，阵风7级；今天最高气温20℃，最低气温15℃，适合在家睡觉与去公园散步，相对湿度65%-90%，台风"黄金"将在48小时内影响我市，请注意，这场台风将给我市吹来大量黄金，请大家关好门窗，以防被黄金砸伤。

（十）、来聊天吧 • Discuss

1. 根据最近的天气预报，告诉你的同学你近期的出游计划。

   Based on recent weather forecasts, tell your classmates whether you have any outdoor activities planned.

2. 告诉你的同学你最喜欢哪个季节，为什么。

   Tell your classmates which season is your favorite and why.

3. 和同学谈谈在不同的天气你会选择去哪里，干什么事。

   Discuss what you do during different types of weather.

第二课 / LESSON 2

你家真漂亮!
YOUR HOME IS REALLY BEAUTIFUL!

这一课我们将学到 • In this lesson we will study the following:
1. 在中国人家做客以及有关爱好方面的内容
2. 重点词语：听说、等……再……、
   哪里哪里、马马虎虎
3. 汉语知识：汉语中的形容词重叠

一、课文 • Text

（在吴帅家里 • In Wu Shuai's home）

 艾美丽： 下午好！
Good afternoon.

 吴帅： 下午好！请进！
Good afternoon. Please come in.

 艾美丽： 你家真漂亮！我能参观一下儿吗？
Your home is really beautiful. Can I look around a bit?

 吴帅： 当然可以，请随便看。
Of course it's all right. Please feel free to look around.

 艾美丽： 你一个人住吗？
Do you live by yourself?

 吴帅： 不，我和朋友一起住，他今天不在。请随便坐。你想喝点儿什么？茶、咖啡，还是其它饮料？
No, I live together with a friend. Today he isn't here. Please feel free to sit. What do you want to drink? Tea? Coffee? Or another drink?

 艾美丽： 我喜欢喝茶，请给我一杯乌龙茶吧。
I'd like to drink tea. Please give me a cup of Wulong tea.

13 • Chinese Without Tears, Advanced Level   Liu Huijun

吴帅： 你挺特别的,一般外国人都不知道乌龙茶。
You are quite unique. Usually foreigners don't know about Wulong tea.

 艾美丽： 是吗?我听我朋友说,广东人很喜欢喝铁观音,我喝了后,也觉得很好喝。
Really? I heard my friends say that Cantonese people really like drinking Tieguanyin. After I drank some, I also thought it was very good.

 吴帅： 你已经是半个广东人了。
You're already half Cantonese.

 艾美丽： 这把二胡是你的吗?
This er-hu, is it yours?

 吴帅： 对,是我的。我上大学以前学过。
It is. It's mine. Before I started college, I studied how to play.

 艾美丽： 你能拉给我听一下儿吗?
Can you play a little for me?

 吴帅： 本来可以,但是现在坏了,不能用了。
Originally I could, but right now it's broken and can't be used.

 艾美丽： 真遗憾!
That's really a pity.

 吴帅： 没关系,等下次修好我再拉给你听。你会什么乐器?
No matter. Wait until the next time it's fixed, and I'll play for you. What instruments can you play?

 艾美丽： 我会弹钢琴,不过水平不高。
I can play piano, but my level is not that high.

 吴帅： 你太谦虚了,一定弹得不错吧?
You're too modest. Surely you play well, right?

 艾美丽： 哪里哪里,马马虎虎。
Not at all. Not at all. So-so.

 吴帅： 吃点儿水果吧,上午在超市买的。多吃点儿,别客气。
Eat a little fruit, OK? I bought it at the supermarket this morning. Eat a little more. There's no need to stand on courtesy.

 艾美丽： 谢谢!
Thanks.

艾美丽要走了 • Emily is about to leave

 艾美丽： 谢谢你今天的款待,我过得很开心。
Thank you for your hospitality today. I spent the time very happily.

 吴帅： 别客气,有空儿常来玩儿。
Don't mention it. Whenever you have time, come have fun.

艾美丽： 再见！请留步！
See you again. I'll see myself out.

吴帅： 再见！慢走！
See you again. Take care.

二、根据课文回答问题 • ANSWER THE FOLLOWING QUESTIONS ACCORDING TO THE TEXT

1. 艾美丽喜欢喝什么饮料？
   _____

2. 吴帅会演奏乐器吗？他会什么乐器？
   _____

3. 艾美丽会演奏乐器吗？她会什么乐器？
   _____

4. 吴帅自己一个人住吗？
   _____

5. 吴帅一般去哪里买东西？
   _____

6. "请留步"是什么意思？
   _____

三、生词 • VOCABULARY

1	朋友	péngyou	名	friend
2	茶	chá	名	tea
3	咖啡	kāfēi	名	coffee
4	其它	qítā	代	other
5	杯	bēi	量	[a measure word, a cup]
6	特别	tèbié	形、副	special, unique; especially, uniquely
7	一般	yìbān	形、副	average, usual; generally, usually
8	听说	tīngshuō	动	to hear of, to hear it said
9	半	bàn	数	half
10	把	bǎ	量	[a measure word, often for furniture or instruments]
11	二胡	èrhú	名	[a Chinese stringed instrument]

12	以前	yǐqián	名	before
13	拉	lā	动	to pull, (of some instruments) to play
14	听	tīng	动	to hear, to listen
15	本来	běnlái	副、形	originally; original
16	坏	huài	形	bad, broken
17	遗憾	yíhàn	形	regretful
18	等……再……	děng……zài……		[see Word Usage]
19	修	xiū	动	to repair, to mend, to fix
20	修理	xiūlǐ	动	to repair, to mend, to fix
21	乐器	yuèqì	名	musical instruments
22	弹	tán	动	(of some musical instruments) to play
23	钢琴	gāngqín	名	piano
24	水平	shuǐpíng	名	level, rank
25	谦虚	qiānxū	形	modest, humble
26	马马虎虎	mǎmǎhūhū		so-so, average, neither good nor bad
27	水果	shuǐguǒ	名	fruit
28	超市	chāoshì	名	supermarket
29	款待	kuǎndài	动	to entertain guests, to act as host
30	过	guò	动	to spend time
31	开心	kāixīn	形	happy
32	空儿	kòngr	名	free time
33	常	cháng	副	often, usually
34	玩儿	wánr	动	to play, to have a good time
35	留步	liúbù		[roughly "I'll see myself out" or "I'll be fine from here"]

专名词 • Proper Names

36	乌龙茶	wūlóngchá		Wulong tea, Oolong tea
37	铁观音	tiěguānyīn		Tieguanyin tea, (Cantonese) Tieh-Kuan-Yin tea

四、词语解释 • Word Usage

（一）、听说

"听说"是"听别人说"的意思，在使用时，如果要说明消息的出处、来源，则要把表示出处、来源的词语放在"听"和"说"之间。

听说 means 听别人说. It is used to indicate a source of information. When indicating a specific source, the source is placed between 听 and 说 (3). It can also be used without a specific source of information (1, 2).

例如：1. 听说明天有一个客人要来。

2. 你听说了这件事吗？
3. 我听玛丽说你生病了。

我们来造句 • Make your own sentence

_____

（二）、可以<u>等</u>下次修好了<u>再</u>弹给你听

"等……再……"常用于表示现在暂时不进行某事，等以后的某个时候或出现某种情况下再进行。

The pattern "等……再……" usually indicates that the moment is not the right time to do something. An appropriate time or a necessary condition is placed after 等.

例如：1. 等放假了再去旅游。
2. 等大学毕业了再去工作。

我们来造句 • Make your own sentence

_____

（三）、哪里哪里

"哪里哪里"常用在被别人夸奖时，表示谦虚、客气。常用在口语，独立成句。也可以只说"哪里"。

哪里哪里 is used to indicate humility when being praised by other people. It is often used in speech and can stand alone as a sentence. It can also be shortened to 哪里.

例如：1. A：你汉语说得真好！
B：哪里哪里。
2. A：你真漂亮！
B：哪里哪里。

我们来造句 • Make your own sentence

_____

（四）、马马虎虎

"马马虎虎"是"马虎"的重叠形式。"马虎"本来的意思是不认真，粗心。重叠后，除了加重语气和程度外，还可以表达水平或程度比较一般的意思。

马马虎虎 is an adjective formed by doubling the adjective 马虎. 马虎 itself means "careless." Doubling the word can not only add emphasis to the original meaning. It can also indicate that a skill, level, or ability is average.

例如：1. 他做事马马虎虎。
2. A：你唱歌唱得真好！
B：哪里哪里，马马虎虎！

我们来造句 • Make your own sentence

五、汉语知识 • Chinese Knowledge

汉语中的形容词重叠 • Doubled adjectives

汉语中的形容词常重叠后使用，重叠后的形容词具有表达加重语气、提高程度以及表示可爱、喜欢等意义和作用。常用的重叠形式有："A→AA的（大→大大的）"、"AB→AABB（马虎→马马虎虎）"、"AB→ABAB（雪白→雪白雪白）"等等。形容词重叠后不能受程度副词的修饰和限制。

Chinese adjectives can often be doubled to add emphasis, to change meanings, or to indicate that a quality is endearing. Single-character adjectives are simply repeated, usually with 的 added to the end. Double-character adjectives can follow an AABB (ex. 马虎 → 马马虎虎) pattern or an ABAB (ex. 雪白→雪白雪白) pattern. Again, 的 is usually added to the end. Doubled adjectives can not be used with intensifiers like 很 or 非常.

例如：1. 老师写的字大大的，最后面的同学也能看清。
2. 我希望你每天都快快乐乐的。
3. 天上的太阳火红火红的。
4. 我今天很高高兴兴。（×）

六、相关链接，与爱好有关的词语 • Related Terms: hobbies

1	爱好	àihào	hobby
2	画画	huàhuàr	painting, drawing
3	看电影	kàndiànyǐng	watching movies
4	看电视	kàndiànshì	watching television
5	看报纸	kànbàozhǐ	reading the newspaper
6	写作	xiězuò	writing, esp. creative writing
7	听音乐	tīngyīnyuè	listening to music
8	玩电脑	wánrdiànnǎo	playing computer games
9	玩网络游戏	wánrwǎngluòyóuxì	playing online games
10	跳舞	tiào//wǔ	dancing
11	骑自行车	qízìxíngchē	bicycling
12	逛街	guàngjiē	shopping
13	旅游	lǚyóu	traveling
14	拉小提琴	lāxiǎotíqín	playing violin
15	弹吉他	tánjítā	playing guitar
16	弹琵琶	tánpípá	playing the pipa (a four-stringed Chinese instrument, similar to a lute)

七、文化生活小贴士 • CULTURAL TIPS: COMMON PHRASES & TIEGUANYIN TEA

(一) 中国人怎么打招呼、聊天儿、告别 • Common phrases in Chinese

▶ 中国人打招呼的时候问："上哪儿去呀？"、"吃饭了吗？"、"怎么这么忙啊？"等等。其实这些话只是普通的打招呼并不是真的要问，所以可以不用回答具体内容。

Many questions in Chinese are not meant to be answered. "上哪去呀?," "吃饭了吗?," and "怎么这么忙啊?" are all simply greetings. Any greeting can be used in response.

▶ "你在哪里发财？"的意思是问你在哪里工作。

"你在哪里发财?" is a common way to ask where someone works.

▶ 告别时，主人常说 "慢走"、"慢点儿骑（自行车）" 之类的话，这并不是真的让客人慢慢走，而是希望客人走好，平安回去的意思。

When seeing guests off, it is common for hosts to say 慢走 or 慢点儿骑 (自行车). Obviously, such sentences do not mean the listener should walk or ride slowly. They simply express the host's wish that guests may return home safely.

(二) 乌龙茶的代表——铁观音 • Tieguanyin tea

▶ 乌龙茶介于绿茶和红茶之间，属于半发酵茶类。铁观音是乌龙茶中有代表性的一种，福建安溪人发明于1725-1735年间。广东人大部分人比较喜欢喝这种茶。

Wulong, or Oolong tea is a semi-fermented tea. It is between a red and a green tea. Tieguanyin, or (Cantonese) Tiehkuanyin, is one type of Wulong tea. It originated in Fujian province's Anxi between 1425 and 1435.

八、练习 • EXERCISES

(一) 填上合适的词语 • Fill in the blanks with appropriate words

去过_____、_____   过得_____、_____

弹　_____、_____   拉_____、_____

修　_____、_____   在_____、_____

（二）选词填空 • Fill in the blanks with the words provided

▶ 参观　　特别　　听说　　遗憾　　谦虚　　款待　　水平　　留步

1. 他这个人很_____，常常一个人在房间里，很少出门。
2. 今天下午王老师要带我们去_____工厂。
3. 因为昨天下雨了，所以没打球，真_____！
4. 吴帅，谢谢你今天的_____。
5. 他的汉语_____很高，像中国人一样。
6. A：慢走，下次再来玩。
   B：好的，请_____。
7. 你太_____了，大家都知道你网球打得很好。
8. _____小王昨天回国了，是真的吗？

▶ 以前　　哪里　　等……再　　一般　　本来

1. 我_____学过钢琴，但是现在不会弹了。
2. 他_____不想吃饭，可看见好吃的又想吃了。
3. 老师还没来，_____老师来了我们_____走吧。
4. A：你一周运动几次？
   B：我_____每周运动三次。
5. A：你汉语说得真好！
   B：_____。

（三）、用所给的词语完成句子 • Answer the questions using the word in parentheses

1. A：你每天几点去学校？
   B：_____。（一般）
2. A：你觉得他怎么样？
   B：_____。（谦虚）
3. A：吴帅今天怎么没来上课？
   B：_____。（听说）
4. A：我觉得这家餐厅的饭不好吃。
   B：_____。（其它）
5. A：我今天有事，不能和你们一起去了。
   B：_____。（遗憾）

（四）、用所学词语表达

Rewrite the following sentences using the provided words or patterns

▶ 等……再

1. 下雨了，不能出门。
   _____

2. 明天有考试，不能去玩儿。
   _____

3. 有点儿不舒服，不能去打球。
   _____

4. 今天没空儿去朋友家。
   _____

▶ 一般

1. 每天八点上课。
   _____

2. 每天在学校的餐厅吃饭。
   _____

3. 每周打三次球。
   _____

4. 每天早上喝咖啡。
   _____

▶ 本来

1. 写对了，改错了。
   _____

2. 准备得很好，但考得不好。
   _____

3. 想去银行取钱，银行关门了。
   _____

4. 想上车，车开走了。
   _____

（五）、词语连接 • Match words to form short phrases

拉　　弹　　打　　踢

钢琴　大提琴　二胡　琵琶　太极拳　足球　排球　乒乓球

（六）、解释下面句中"还"及与"还"有关的词语的意思或用法

Explain what 还 means in each of the following sentences

1. A: 你喝咖啡**还是**喝果汁？
   B: **还是**喝咖啡吧。

2. 交完钱以后**还要**买书。
3. **还**记得我吗？我们在机场见过。
4. 你如果**还有**问题请问老师吧。
5. 已经下午两点了，他**还**没吃饭呢。

（七）、连接两个合适的句子

Match the sentences on the left to appropriate responses on the right

A：你真漂亮！　　　　　B：很开心。

A：你汉语说得怎么样？　　B：马马虎虎。

A：你今天过得怎么样？　　B：请留步。

A：慢走！　　　　　　　　B：哪里哪里。

（八）、角色扮演 • Performance

两人一组，一个扮演主人，一个扮演客人，用课文中的词语进行会话练习。

Work in pairs. One student plays the host, while the other plays the guest. Prepare a dialogue using the words in the text.

（九）、来聊天吧 • Discuss

▶ 1. 在你的国家，去朋友家做客一般送什么礼物？应该注意哪些问题？

In your country, do you give any gifts when you go to a friend's home? If so, what kinds of presents are given? What etiquette do visitors observe in your country?

▶ 2. 你喜欢什么饮料？为什么？

What do you like to drink? Why?

▶ 3. 谈谈你的业余爱好

Talk about your hobbies

1. 你喜欢看电影还是喜欢看电视？
2. 你喜欢和朋友一起去唱歌吗？为什么？
3. 你喜欢看哪本书？为什么？
4. 有什么书或电影你愿意看多几遍？
5. 你喜欢哪部电影？为什么？
6. 你喜欢哪幅画？为什么？
7. 你喜欢旅游吗？为什么？
8. 你喜欢去哪里旅游？

第三课
LESSON 3

你要租房子吗?
YOU WANT TO RENT AN APARTMENT?

这一课我们将学到 • In this lesson we will study the following:
1. 怎样租房子
2. 重点词语：……是……，就是……、算、到时、只要……就……
3. 辨析："房主"和"房东"
4. 汉语知识：汉语中约数的表达

一、课文 • Text

(在房地产中介公司 • In a real estate office)

 中介人员： 小姐，你好！请问，你要租房吗？
Miss, hello. May I ask whether you want to rent an apartment?

 艾美丽： 是，我想租一套离深圳大学近一点儿的房子，你有吗？
I do. I want to rent an apartment relatively close to Shenzhen University. Do you have any?

 中介人员： 有啊，你想租多大的？
We do have some. How large an apartment do you want to rent?

 艾美丽： 不要太大。
I don't need anything too big.

 中介人员： 那你看看这套一房一厅的。
Then look at this one-fang, one-ting apartment.

 艾美丽： 一房一厅的是什么意思？
What does "one-fang, one ting" mean?

 中介人员： 就是一间卧室，一间客厅，另外还有卫生间和厨房。
That is one bedroom and one sitting room. Aside from those it has a bathroom and kitchen.

艾美丽： 有阳台吗？我喜欢带阳台的。
Does it have a balcony? I would like one with a balcony.

中介人员： 那你看看这套60平米的，这套带阳台。
Then look at this 60-square-meters one. This one has a balcony.

艾美丽： 这套房租很贵吗？
Is this apartment's rent very expensive?

中介人员： 因为这个公寓带电梯，而且房子朝阳，所以有点儿贵。
Because this building has an elevator, also because the apartment faces the sun, it's a bit expensive.

艾美丽： 住这儿方便吗？
Is living here convenient?

中介人员： 很方便，中国餐馆和便利店就在楼下。学校离这儿不远，走路差不多八、九分钟就到了。
It's very convenient. There are a Chinese restaurant and a convenience store downstairs. The campus is not far from here. If you walk about eight or nine minutes, you're there.

艾美丽： 这套月租金是多少？
This apartment's monthly rent is how much?

中介人员： 两千八百元。
2, 800 yuan.

艾美丽： 家电、家具都有吗？
Does it have all the appliances and furniture?

中介人员： 家电、家具齐全，而且是精装修。
It is fully furnished. In addition, it is well-decorated.

艾美丽： 好是好，就是有点儿贵。
Nice is nice, it's just a bit expensive.

中介人员： 不算贵了，如果你真想租，我们还可以跟房主商量一下儿，稍微便宜点儿。
It's not considered expensive. If you really want to rent it, we can discuss it with the owner, get the cost a bit less expensive.

艾美丽： 中介费怎么收？
How about the finder's fee?

中介人员： 月租金的一半。
It's half of a month's rent.

艾美丽： 房租怎么交？
How would I pay the rent?

 中介人员： 先交一个月押金，以后每月月底交下一个月的租金。到时房东会给你个银行账号，你只要把钱存到这个账户上就可以了。
First, you pay one month's deposit. Then, at every month's end, you pay one month's rent. At the time you sign the lease, the landlord will give you a bank account number. You just take the rent money and deposit it in this bank account. Then it's OK.

 艾美丽： 什么时候可以去看房子？
When can we go to see the apartment?

 中介人员： 我们先跟房主商量一下儿，到时打电话给你，可以吗？
First we'll consult with the owner. Once that's done, we'll call you, OK?

 艾美丽： 可以。这是我的电话号码。
All right. This is my phone number.

 中介人员： 那好，我们再联系。
Then, good. We'll contact you again.

 艾美丽： 嗯，好的，再见！
Umm, OK. See you again.

二、根据课文回答问题 • ANSWER THE FOLLOWING QUESTIONS ACCORDING TO THE TEXT

1. 艾美丽想租一套什么样的房子？
   _____

2. 一房一厅是什么意思？
   _____

3. 艾美丽喜欢什么样的房子？
   _____

4. 中介公司的中介费怎么收？
   _____

5. 房租怎么交？
   _____

三、生词 • VOCABULARY

#	词	拼音	词性	英文
1	租	zū	动	to rent
2	房子	fángzi	名	apartment
3	房地产	fángdìchǎn	名	real estate
4	中介	zhōngjiè	名	intermediary
5	人员	rényuán	名	worker
6	中介人员	zhōngjièrényuán		middle man, intermediary
7	套	tào	量	[a measure word for sets or apartments]
8	离	lí	介	from
9	近	jìn	形	near
10	房（间）	fáng（jiān）	名	room
11	厅	tīng	名	lobby, hall, room
12	意思	yìsi	名	meaning, definition
13	间	jiān	量	[a measure word for rooms]
14	卧室	wòshì	名	bedroom
15	客厅	kètīng	名	sitting room, living room
16	另外	lìngwài	副	besides, in addition
17	卫生间	wèishēngjiān	名	washroom, bathroom
18	厨房	chúfáng	名	kitchen
19	阳台	yángtái	名	balcony
20	平（方）米	píng（fāng）mǐ	量	[a measure word, a square meter]
21	房租	fángzū		rent money
22	贵	guì	形	expensive
23	公寓	gōngyù	名	apartment building
24	电梯	diàntī	名	elevator, lift
25	朝	cháo	介	facing
26	阳（太阳）	yáng（tàiyáng）	名	the Sun
27	方便	fāngbiàn	形	convenient
28	餐馆	cānguǎnr	名	restaurant
29	便利	biànlì	形	convenient
30	便利店	biànlìdiàn	名	convenience store
31	楼	lóu	名、量	floor, story, a storied building
32	下（面）	xià（mian）	名	down (bottom)
33	走路	zǒulù	名	to walk
34	差不多	chàbuduō	副	almost, nearly, just about
35	九	jiǔ	数	nine
36	租金	zūjīn	名	rent money
37	千	qiān	数	thousand
38	家具	jiājù	名	furniture
39	家电	jiādiàn	名	electrical appliance
40	齐全	qíquán	形	complete, fully equipped
41	精	jīng	形	fine, excellent
42	装修	zhuāngxiū	动	to decorate
43	算	suàn	动	to be considered

44	房主	fángzhǔ	名	owner
45	商量	shāngliang	动	to discuss, to talk about
46	稍微	shāowēi	副	a little
47	押金	yājīn	名	deposit
48	底	dǐ	名	the end of
49	时	shí	名	a point in time, moment
50	到时	dàoshí		at a specific time
51	房东	fángdōng	名	landlord
52	账号	zhànghào	名	account number
53	只要……就……	zhǐyào……jiù……		[see Word Usage]
54	存	cún	动	to deposit, to save, to keep
55	账户	zhànghù	名	account
56	时候	shíhou	名	time
57	联系	liánxì	动	to contact

专名词 • Proper Names

| 58 | 中国 | zhōngguó | | China |

四、词语解释 • Word Usage

（一）、好**是**好，**就是**有点儿贵

"……是……，就是……"的意思是肯定某种情况或某种说法，但同时指出与前面情况或说法不同的内容。常用来表达对事物的某一方面不满意的意思。"……是……"表示让步，"就是"在这里是"只是"的意思。

The pattern "…是…，就是…" is used to affirm a situation or opinion while at the same time raising a contradictory point. "…是…" indicates the point of affirmation. 就是, here, is the same as 只是, and it often precedes a point of dissatisfaction.

例如：1. 这件衣服好是好，就是你穿有点儿大。
2. 四川菜好吃是好吃，就是太辣了。

我们来造句 • Make your own sentence

_____

（二）、不**算**贵了

在这里，"算"的意思是表示没达到但又很接近某种情况或某种程度，带有勉强的语气。

Here, 算 indicates a scenario or quality has nearly been, but not yet been, reached. It is often used for emphasis.

例如：1. 吃一个面包就算是吃饭了。
2. 这次考试不算太难。

我们来造句 • Make your own sentence

（三）、<u>到时</u>房东会给你一个银行账号

"到时"的意思是"到那个时候"，是指交流双方都明白的未来的某个时间或发生某种事情的时候。也可以说"到时候"。

倒是 has the same meaning as 到那个时候. It indicates a future time or situation that both the speaker and the listener can understand. 到时候 can be used the same way.

例如：1. 我下个月回来，到时我会给你带礼物的。
2. 我现在也没想好怎么办，我到时再告诉你。
3. 下课以后我就有时间了，到时候我们可以好好聊。
4. 欢迎你去我家，到时候我给你包饺子吃。

我们来造句 • Make your own sentence

_____

（四）、只要……就……

汉语中，"只要……就……"表达的意思是，满足前一句条件的情况下，可以出现后一句中的情况。

The pattern "只要…就…" indicates that whenever one condition is fulfilled, a second situation will occur.

例如：1. 只要天气好，我们就去外面玩。
2. 只要见到你，我就开心。

我们来造句 • Make your own sentence

_____

○ 辨析：Distinguish between the following words

☞ "房主"和"房东"

"房主"是"房子的主人"的意思，"房东"是把自己房子租给别人的人。"房主"不一定是"房东"，但"房东"一定是"房主"。在使用时，可以说"他是我的房东。"意思是：他是房子的主人，我租他的房子。但不能说"他是我的房主。"（✕）而只能说"他是这套房子的房主。"

房主 refers to the owner of a property. 房东 refers to the person renting one property to another. An owner (房主) is not necessarily a landlord (房东), but by law, a landlord is the owner of said property. "他是我的房东" is correct, as is "他是这套房子的房主." However, "他是我的房主" is incorrect.

○ 课文注释：Key Points in the Text

☞ "到时打电话给你"

这句话标准的语序是"到时我给你打电话。"但在现实生活中，越来越多的人说"我打电话给你"，或者"给你电话"，为了让对话更自

然,也为了方便学生在生活中使用,就从俗,写成了"打电话给你"。

Strictly speaking, the word order in this sentence should be 到时我给你打电话. However, in common speech, it is increasingly common to say 我打电话给你 or 给你电话. Therefore, in order to make the conversation more natural and applicable to daily use, the common 打电话给你 is used here.

五、汉语知识 • Chinese Knowledge

汉语中约数的表达 • Approximate numbers

汉语中,常用两个从小到大相邻的数字表达大约、大概的数量、时间等。

Chinese often uses two adjacent numbers to indicate approximate quantities or times.

例如: 1. 只要八、九分钟就到了。
2. 他大概十三、四岁。
3. 大概去了二、三十个人。

六、相关链接,与租房有关的词语 • Related Terms: rentals

1	租客	zūkè	tenant, renter
2	配套设施	pèitàoshèshī	additional facilities
3	户型	hùxíng	style of home
4	签	qiān	to sign
5	合同	hétong	contract

七、文化生活小贴士 • Tips for Daily Life: dormitory & ADSL

(一)、深圳大学留学生楼 • International Students' Dormitory

深圳大学留学生楼位于文山湖畔。一共有双人房54间,单人房167间。房间有卫生间、热水器、电视机、冰箱、空调和互联网端口。留学生楼有会议厅、阅览室、咖啡厅、洗衣房和聚会庭院。

Shenzhen University's International Students' Dormitory is beside Wenshan Lake. It has 54 double and 167 single rooms. Each has a rest room, water heater, television, refrigerator, air-conditioner and Internet socket. The building has a conference room, reading rooms, a café, a laundry, and nearby courtyards for social gatherings.

（二）、如何开通校园网及宽带 • ADSL

How to open a campus network account and set up a broadband account

（1）开通校园网：请带上学生证到科技楼809（电话：26537109）开户。

（2）住在留学生楼的学生开通宽带ADSL：请带上护照和银行卡复印件到留学生楼办公室C101申请。

(1) Bring your student card to room 809 of the Science and Technology building to open a campus network account.

(2) Bring your passport and a copy of your bank card to Room C101 of the International Students' Building to open a broadband account.

八、练习 • Exercises

（一）、填上合适的词语 • Fill in the blanks with appropriate words

租 _____、_____、_____租

中介 _____、_____、_____齐全

带 _____、 交_____、

（二）、选词填空 • Fill in the blanks with the words provided

▶ 算　　存　　差不多　　装修　　稍微　　商量　　联系　　方便

1. 这个字和那个字_____，所以我常写错。
2. 这家餐馆的菜还可以，不_____贵，
3. 买房比把钱_____在银行好。
4. 我不知道选择哪一套房好，想回家_____一下儿。
5. 住在留学生宿舍挺_____的。
6. 你有事就给我打电话，希望常常_____。
7. 老师还没下课，请_____等一下儿。
8. 他的家_____得很漂亮。

▶ 房东　　房主

1. 我把这个月的房租交给我的_____了。
2. _____不在，没办法看房子，只好下次再来。
3. 我来介绍一下儿：这位是我的_____张先生。
4. 我们不是朋友，他是_____，我是租客。

（三）、用所给词语完成句子 • Fill in the blanks with sentences using the words given in parentheses

1. A: 从你家到学校多长时间？
   B: _____。（走路）

2. A：你要去中国留学吗？
   B：_____。（商量）

3. A：你会打太极拳吗？
   B：_____。（算）

4. A：我怎么能找到你？
   B：_____。（到时）

5. A：你想去超市买什么？
   B：_____。（另外）

（四）、使用划线词语仿造例句造句 • Use the underlined words to form sentences

1. <u>只要</u>把钱存到房东的账户上<u>就</u>可以了。_____
2. 我的宿舍<u>离</u>学校很近。_____
3. 这套房子租金很贵，<u>差不多</u>三千块。_____
4. 我不知道去哪儿玩儿好，我要<u>跟</u>大家<u>商量</u>一下儿。_____
5. 我经常<u>跟</u>朋友电话<u>联系</u>。_____
6. 好<u>是</u>好，<u>就是</u>太贵了。_____

（五）、解释下面句中"下"的意思或用法

Explain the meaning of 下 in the following sentences

1. <u>下</u>车以后往右走。
2. 我们每天12点<u>下</u>课。
3. 走到他家门口，我按<u>下</u>了门铃。
4. 各位乘客：<u>下</u>一站是深圳大学。
5. 请等一<u>下</u>儿，我要记录一<u>下</u>儿。
6. 欢迎您<u>下</u>次乘坐本公司的出租车。
7. 便利店就在楼<u>下</u>。
8. 今天<u>下</u>雨了。
9. 今天天气很冷，零<u>下</u>十五度。

（六）、用所学词语表达 • Rewrite the sentences using the words provided

▶ 差不多

1. 三点五十分。
2. 两件衣服的款式很像。
3. 坐公交车35分钟，坐出租30分钟。
4. "太"字和"大"字

▶ ……是……，就是
1. 裙子很漂亮，但贵。
2. 房子不错，但离学校远。
3. 汉语很有意思，但难。
4. 天气晴，但有风。

▶ 算
1. 从你家到学校走十五分钟。
2. 原价230元，打折后200元。
3. 跟他学汉语，但他是你朋友。
4. 学了一年钢琴，会一点儿。

（七）、根据所给材料练习 • Performance

1. 两位同学分别扮演房东和租客，进行问答练习。

   Work in pairs. One student plays a landlord. The other plays a tenant. Prepare a conversation.

2. 下面两套房子你想租哪一套，说出原因。

   Which of the following homes would you want to rent? Why?

租房广告
2000/月 南苑新村两房一厅
面积：90平米
装修：简装修
朝向：朝南
楼层：5/7
配套设施：水、电、有线电视；带家具
地址：南山大道与南光路交汇处

芳华苑
户型：一房一厅
面积：60平米
房租：1500/月
楼层：0/7
朝向：朝阳
地址：南山华侨城世界之窗对面

（八）、来聊天吧 • Discuss

1. 跟大家说一说你住哪儿、方便不方便。

   Tell everyone where you live. Is it convenient?

2. 你住的是什么房子？跟大家说一说。

   What kind of home do you live in?

3. 介绍一下你房间有什么家具和家电。

   Tell everyone about the furniture and appliances in your home.

（九）、写出图中房间中设施或物品的名称

Write the names of the furniture and appliances you can see in the following pictures

现代韩式卧室

墨西哥卧室

东南亚中户型卫生间

第四课 能不能便宜点儿?
LESSON 4 CAN YOU SELL IT ANY CHEAPER?

这一课我们将学到 • In this lesson we will study the following:
1. 怎样讨价还价
2. 重点词语：怎么可能、这我都不赚钱、要不、才、最多、谁说的、不行就算了、好了
3. 汉语知识：汉语中的反问句

一、课文 • Text

（艾美丽在东门白马和店主讨价还价 • Emily haggles with a shopkeeper in Dongmen Baima）

 店主： 嘿！进来看一看哪，甩卖啦，便宜啦！(看见艾美丽：欢迎光临！)
Hey! Come on in and have a look. Clearance sale! Really inexpensive! (Sees Emily: "Welcome here.")

 艾美丽： 这双鞋多少钱？
This pair of shoes (costs) how much?

 店主： 280。
280.

 艾美丽： 太贵了，能不能便宜点儿？150怎么样？
That's too expensive. Can you sell it any cheaper? How about 150?

 店主： 150？怎么可能？这我都不赚钱，150块我赔死了。
150? How is that possible? I'm already not making money. At 150 RMB, I'd take a huge loss.

 艾美丽： 别骗人了，你以为我不知道这双鞋的成本哪！
Don't try to fool people. You think I don't know this pair of shoes' production cost?

 店主： 哎呀，现在生意不好做呀！
Ai-ya! Right now business is no good!

艾美丽： 那不行，我不要了。
Then, no good. I don't want them now.

店主: 要不你多买一双怎么样？我给你便宜点儿。
How about if you buy one more pair? I'll give you a little cheaper price.

艾美丽: 不行，我朋友买了一样的才140，我最多给155。
No good. My friend bought the same pair for only 140. At most I'll give you 155.

店主: 谁说的？再加一点儿吧，160怎么样？
Says who? Add a bit more, OK? How about 160?

艾美丽: 155。不行就算了。
155. If that's no good, then forget it.

艾美丽转身走开 • Emily turns and walks away

店主: 回来，回来！
Come back, come back!

艾美丽: 155行不行？
Is 155 OK or not?

店主: 好了，好了，拿走吧。你太厉害了！
OK, OK, take them and go, OK? You're too skilled at haggling!

艾美丽: 给你钱。
Here is your money.

店主: 这是200，找你45，对吧。
This is 200. I give you 45 as change, right?

艾美丽: 对。谢谢。这张20的太旧了，换一张。
Right. Thanks. This 20 yuan bill is too old. Change it for another.

店主: 好吧，换一张。
OK, I'll change it.

艾美丽: 这张是真的吗？像假的。
Is this bill real? It seems fake.

店主: 不会啦，肯定是真的啦。
Not possible. Certainly it is real.

艾美丽: 好吧。
OK.

店主: 好啦，谢谢啦，再来啊！
OK, thanks. Come again.

艾美丽: 好，谢谢，再见！
Good, thanks. See you again.

二、根据课文回答问题 • ANSWER THE FOLLOWING QUESTIONS ACCORDING TO THE TEXT

1. 280元的鞋，艾美丽多少钱买下了？
   _____

2. 店主建议艾美丽怎么做？艾美丽做了吗？
   _____

3. 艾美丽为什么说店主骗人？
   _____

4. 艾美丽为什么要店主便宜点儿卖给她？
   _____

5. 你觉得艾美丽在讨价还价方面是不是很厉害？
   _____

三、生词 • VOCABULARY

1	店主	diànzhǔ	名	store owner, shopkeeper
2	讨价还价	tǎojiàhuánjià		to haggle, to argue over prices
3	甩	shuǎi	动	to throw, to discard
4	甩卖	shuǎimài		clearance sale
5	啦	la	助	[combination of 了 and 啊, used to indicate exclamations]
6	光临	guānglín	动	to be present, to be in a place
7	双	shuāng	量	pair
8	鞋	xié	名	shoes
9	赚	zhuàn	动	to make a profit
10	赔	péi	动	to stand a loss
11	……死了	……sǐle	…	extremely
12	骗	piàn	动	to fool, to lie, to cheat
13	以为	yǐwéi	动	to think, to assume
14	成本	chéngběn	名	cost
15	生意	shēngyi	名	business
16	行	xíng	形	OK, acceptable, able
17	要不	yàobu		[see Word Usage]
18	才	cái	副	only

19	加	jiā	动	to add
20	算了	suànle		"Forget it"
21	厉害	lìhai	形	[generally indicates an extremely high degree or ability, for both positive traits and negative traits; in most dictionaries, "ferocious" or "terrible"; can also be roughly translated as "great" or "awe-inspiring"]
22	找（钱）	zhǎo（qián）	动	to give change
23	张	zhāng	量	[a measure word, usually for flat objects]
24	旧	jiù	形	old
25	假	jiǎ	形	fake, false, counterfeit
26	肯定	kěndìng	形、副	sure, certain; surely, certainly

专名词 • Proper Names

| 27 | 东门白马 | dōngménbáimǎ | | Dongmen Baima |

四、词语解释 • WORD USAGE

（一）、<u>怎么</u>可能？

在这里，"怎么"不是普通的疑问词，而是表达反问的语气，"怎么可能？"的意思不是问"可能吗"、"通过什么方式可以做到"，而是说"不可能。"

Here, 怎么 is not a literal question, but a rhetorical question. "怎么可能？" is not asking in what way something might be possible. It is stating that something is not possible.

例如：1. 我怎么知道？（意思是：我不知道。）

2. 我怎么能不知道？（意思是：我知道。）

我们来造句 • Make your own sentence

_____

（二）、这我<u>都</u>不赚钱

在这里，"都"表示某种情况发生了，相当于"已经"的意思，含有强调的语气。句尾常出现"了"。出现在数量词前，常表示时间晚、数量多、年龄大等。

Here, 都 is comparable to 已经 and indicates a situation has already occurred. It is used for emphasis. When it appears before numbers, it usually indicates a late time, a large quantity, or old age.

例如：1. 我都知道了，你别说了。

2. 都十二点了，快睡觉吧。

3. 他都二十八了，应该结婚了。

我们来造句 • Make your own sentence

（三）、<u>要不</u>你多买一双怎么样？

在这里，"要不"表示建议的意思。多用于口语，常出现在句首。

Here, 要不 is used to indicate a suggestion. It is used in speech and appears at the beginning of clauses.

例如： 1. 要不我们去吃四川菜怎么样？
　　　 2. 要不你坐出租车去吧。

我们来造句 • Make your own sentence

（四）、我朋友买了一样的<u>才</u>140元

在这里，"才"出现在数量词前，表示时间早、数量少、年龄小、程度低等意思。多用于表达说话人的主观感觉。

When 才 appears before numbers, it indicates an early time, a low quantity, a young age, or a low degree. It most often expresses the speaker's personal opinion.

例如： 1. 别着急，才五点。
　　　 2. 他才十二岁。
　　　 3. 这件衣服很便宜，才300多块。

我们来造句 • Make your own sentence

（五）、我<u>最多</u>给155元

在这里，"最"和"多"一起使用，组成"最多"，表示最大限度。意思是"不会超过……"。常出现在表示时间、数量的词语前。"最"还可以和其它形容词一起，组成"最+形容词"的格式，表示限制程度、时间、数量、范围等。比如"最大"、"最小"、"最少"、"最远"、"最近"、"最早"、"最晚"等等。

Here, 最 and 多 are used together to form 最多. It indicates a maximum limit and often appears before times or quantities. 最 can be used with many other adjectives to form similar words that limit degree, time, or scope, such as 最大, 最小, 最少, 最远, 最早, and 最晚.

例如： 1. 我最早七点到。
　　　 2. 这套房最多有80平米。
　　　 3. 我觉得他最小二十四岁。
　　　 4. 我开车最远到过广州。

我们来造句 • Make your own sentence

（六）、<u>谁说的</u>？

在这里，"谁"不是普通的疑问，而是反问，意思是"没有谁"、"谁也不"。"谁说的"的意思是"没有谁说"，也就是"没有人说"、"你说的不对"的意思。

Here, 谁 does not indicate a literal question, but a rhetorical one. It means no one. "谁说的?" means the same as "没有人说" or "你说的不对."

例如：1. 谁知道他去哪儿了？（意思是：没人知道他去哪儿了）
      2. A：你喝我的咖啡了？
         B：谁喝你的咖啡了？（意思是：我没喝你的咖啡）

我们来造句 • Make your own sentence

_____

（七）、不行就<u>算了</u>

在这里，"算了"是表达阻止或停止事情、谈话继续下去的意思。常含有不满、勉强或无可奈何的意思。常用于口语。可出现在句尾，也可独立成句。

Here, 算了 indicates the end of a matter or conversation. It often shows dissatisfaction or a lack of options. It is frequently used in speech. It can be used at the end of a sentence or stand alone as a sentence.

例如：1. 你不说算了。
      2. 你不去就算了，我自己去吧。
      3. 算了，你别说了。

我们来造句 • Make your own sentence

_____

（八）、<u>好了</u>，<u>好了</u>，拿走吧

在这里，"好了"、"好了，好了"表示阻止事情、谈话继续下去的意思，常含有不满或无可奈何的语气。而单独使用"好了"表示主动停止或结束某事时，则不含有不满的意思。常用语口语。

Here, "好了, 好了" also indicates the end of a matter or conversation. It often shows dissatisfaction or a lack of options. However, using a single 好了 alone simply signals the end of the matter, without necessarily indicating dissatisfaction (3). It is frequently used in speech.

例如：1. 好了，你别说了。
      2. 好了，好了，就听你的，去打网球吧。
      3. 好了，今天的课就上到这儿。

我们来造句 • Make your own sentence

_____

五、汉语知识 • Chinese Knowledge

汉语中的反问句 • Rhetorical Questions in Chinese

汉语中，常用一些疑问词来表达反问的语气，在这种情况下，普通的疑问词并不表达普通疑问的语气，而是反问的语气，也就是表面看是疑问，但表达的意思却是确定的。比如："怎么可能？"的意思并不是普通的问"可能吗"、"通过什么方式可以做到"。而是说"不可能。"判断一个句子是普通的疑问句还是反问句要根据具体的语言环境来判断。反问句可以表达肯定的意思，也可以表达否定的意思。为了方便，在理解句意的时候，我们可以把句中的疑问词看成是一个否定的词。

例如："谁知道？"就是"不知道"。而"谁不知道？"就是"都知道。"

Rhetorical questions are commonly used in Chinese. They are, of course, not meant to be answered. Rather, they are used to show certainty or confirmation. For example "怎么可能？" is not asking in what way something might be possible. It is stating that something is not possible.

Whether a question is literal or rhetorical must be determined by its place in a specific conversation. Often, using the negative response to a question word can help to understand the meaning of a rhetorical question. For example, changing 谁 in "谁知道?"and "谁不知道?" to 没有人 can help understand the questions' meanings of "没有人知道," and "没有人不知道," respectively. These can then be further simplified to "不知道" and "都知道," respectively.

六、相关链接 • Related Terms: prices

1	砍价	kǎn//jià	to reduce prices, to ask for lower prices
2	杀价	shā//jià	to force a seller to sell at a lower price
3	一口价	yìkǒujià	a fixed price
4	清仓	qīngcāng	to take inventory of a warehouse
5	转行	zhuǎnháng	(of work) to change fields

七、文化生活小贴士 • Cultural Links: Shenzhen shopping areas

（一）、深圳的主要商业区 Shenzhen's major retail areas

▶ 罗湖东门

东门商业步行街区，总占地面积17.6万平方米，28栋现代化大型商厦分布在15条主要街道上，是集旅游观光、饮食休闲、购物消费为一体的标志性商业街区。

Dongmen Commercial Pedestrian Street occupies a footprint of 176,000 square meters. It includes 28 modern retail buildings and is spread over 15 streets. It is a major center for the travel industry, entertainment industry, restaurants and retail.

Bus: 公交 - 113路空调，出发：深圳大学，下车站：东门，Taxi: 70元左右

▶ 华强北

华强北商业区位于深圳，其前身主要是生产电子产品的中心区，是深圳最传统、最具人气的商业旺地之一。

The retail area of Huaqiangbei is among the oldest and most popular shopping areas in Shenzhen. It is a major retail area for electronic goods.

  Bus：公交 – 113路空调，出发：深圳大学，下车站：上海宾馆站

  Taxi：50元左右，Metro：出发：深圳大学，下车站：华强路

八、练习 · Exercises

（一）、填上合适的词语 · Fill in the blanks with appropriate words

加_____、_____ 骗_____、_____

最_____、_____ _____、_____死了

欢迎_____ 讨价_____

（二）、选词填空 · Fill in the blanks with the words provided

▶ 再　怎么　算了　好了　都　……死了　要不　才

1. 房租贵_____，我不租了。
2. 你不去_____！我自己去。
3. 我今天没空儿，_____我们明天去吧。
4. 她_____会不来？我想她会来的。
5. _____，就听你的吧。
6. 这件衣服有点儿肥，_____瘦一点儿就好了。
7. 这台电脑很便宜，_____2000块钱。
8. 今天_____星期三了，再过两天就周末了。

▶ 加　以为　成本　生意　骗　厉害　赚　赔　店主　甩卖　光临

1. 这件衣服的_____只有20块钱，可商店里要卖150块。
2. _____上妈妈给的钱一共是3600块。
3. 我_____今天会下雨，所以带了雨伞，可是没下。
4. 她讨价还价很_____，本来说200块钱的，她50块就买下了。
5. 年底超市在大_____，我们也去看看怎么样？
6. 他经常_____人，所以大家都不相信他了。
7. 我也不知道多少钱，等_____回来再说吧。
8. 他20岁就到外面做_____去了。
9. 他把在深圳_____的钱都给妈妈了，自己从不花钱。
10. 他以为能赚大钱，可是最后把钱都_____进去了。
11. 欢迎_____！请里面坐。

（三）、用所给词语完成句子 • Fill in the blanks with sentences using the words given in parentheses

1. A：我不知道坐几路公交车。
   B：_____。（算了）

2. A：几点了？
   B：_____。（都）

3. A：这套房子有多大？
   B：_____。（最多）

4. A：你学了多长时间汉语了？
   B：_____。（才）

5. A：这个问题我也不会。
   B：_____。（要不）

6. A：这是你写的吗？
   B：_____。（肯定）

7. A：你朋友小提琴拉得怎么样？
   B：_____。（厉害）

8. A：今天天气怎么样？
   B：_____。（……死了）

（四）、用所学词语表达 • Rewrite the sentences using the words provided

▶ 怎么
1. 不相信今天的温度是26度。
2. 东西太贵了。
3. 不相信有考试。
4. 一个小时太少了，做不完。

▶ 才
1. 觉得东西太便宜。
2. 觉得时间太少。
3. 觉得距离太近。
4. 觉得气温很低。

▶ 要不
1. 建议朋友买一件红色的裙子。
2. 建议朋友去吃四川菜。
3. 同学身体不舒服，你怎么说？
4. 同学在等你，可你的事还没做完。

▶ 最多
1. 从你的家到学校需要30——40分钟。
2. 你觉得朋友买的衣服应该在200——300元之间。
3. 你觉得她在30岁到34之间。
4. 你想在中国住一年到两年。

（五）、填量词 • Fill in the blanks with the appropriate measure word

家　套　间　把　杯　件　位　瓶　条　种　块　张

一_____饭馆　　一_____裤子　　一_____咖啡　　一_____卧室

一_____老师　　一_____衣服　　一_____吉他　　一_____水果

一_____钱　　　一_____票　　　一_____酒　　　一_____房

（六）、做游戏 • Play a game

老师先在黑板上写下各种商品的原价，如苹果，牛奶，衬衫等。然后把班上的同学分成顾客和商人。再把商人分成三人一组，每一组是一个商店，卖黑板上提供的东西。然后给每个顾客发50元纸做的假币。让商店里的商人记下每一笔收入，让每一位顾客记下每一笔支出。另外要求顾客向商人讨价还价。最后老师统计每个商店赚了多少，每个顾客所买的东西花了多少钱，赚得最多的商店和买的东西最便宜的顾客算是赢家。

The teacher will write wholesale prices for a number of sales items on the board. Students will be divided into salespeople and customers. Salespeople will work in groups of three to "run" a store. Customers will each be given 50 "RMB." Customers will then try to buy sales items for the lowest possible price. Everyone should write down any transactions. The "store" that makes the most money and the customer who gets the lowest prices win.

（七）、角色扮演 • Performance

两位同学分别扮演售货员和顾客，进行讨价还价的练习。

Students work in pairs. One plays a salesperson, while the other plays a customer. Prepare a conversation.

（八）、商店打折了 • Stores have marked down their prices

商店打折了！你想去哪间商店呢？你打算买哪双鞋子？哪间店折扣最低？你认为哪一双鞋最便宜最好看，为什么？

Two stores are having sales. What store do you want to go to? Which pair of shoes do you want to buy? Which store is offering the largest discount? Which store do you think has the least expensive and best looking shoes? Why?

商店一：

商店二：

（九）、来聊天吧 • Discuss

1. 你会讨价还价吗？向同学介绍讨价还价的方法。

   Are you able to haggle? Tell your classmates any good approaches you know for haggling.

2. 讲一个有关买东西的有趣的故事。

   Tell a story about an interesting experience you've had while shopping.

第五课 / LESSON 5

我房间的水龙头坏了
MY ROOM'S FAUCET IS BROKEN

这一课我们将学到 • In this lesson we will study the following:
1. 你的家用电器坏了怎么办
2. 重点词语：该……了、……以内、正好
3. 辨析："维修"和"修理"、"保修"和"报修"
4. 汉语知识：汉语中可能或不可能的表达

一、课文 • Text

（艾美丽给宿舍管理处打电话 • Emily gives the dormitory management office a phone call）

艾美丽： 你好，是宿舍管理处吗？
Hello. Is this the dormitory management office?

宿舍管理员： 是。有什么事？
It is. What matter do you have?

艾美丽： 你好，我房间的水龙头坏了，麻烦您帮我修一下儿好吗？
Hello. My room's faucet is broken. Can I trouble you to help me get it fixed?

宿舍管理员： 你住哪个房间？
You live in which room?

艾美丽： 205房间。
Room 205.

宿舍管理员： 水龙头怎么了？
What's wrong with the faucet?

艾美丽： 总是关不紧，漏水。
It's always impossible to turn off completely and leaks water.

宿舍管理员： 好的，我们马上派人去修。
OK. We'll immediately send someone to go fix it.

艾美丽： 好，谢谢！
Good. Thanks.

维修员来到艾美丽宿舍 • The repairman arrives at Emily's room

维修员： （敲门）：你好，请问是你这里的水龙头坏了吗？
Hello, may I ask whether it is here the faucet is broken?

艾美丽： 嗯，是。请进，请帮我看一下儿。
Umm, it is. Please come in. Please check it for me.

维修员： （检查后）你的水龙头该换了，我帮你换一个新的好吗？
(After checking the faucet) Your faucet needs to be replaced. I'll help you replace it with a new one, OK?

艾美丽： 大概多少钱？
About how much money?

维修员： 水龙头20块，加上修理费10块，一共是30块。
The faucet is 20 RMB. Adding on the repair fee of 10 RMB, altogether it's 30 RMB.

艾美丽： 好，那你帮我换一个吧。
Ok, then replace it with a new one, OK?

维修员： 好的。
OK.

维修员换好水龙头 • The repairman has replaced the faucet

维修员： 好的，可以了，请试一下儿。
OK, it's fine. Please try it out.

艾美丽： 嗯。（艾美丽试完水龙头）好了，谢谢您！这是30块钱，您数一数。
Umm (Emily tries the faucet), OK. Thank you. Here is 30 RMB. Please count it.

维修员： 好的，正好30块。我帮你开一张收据。
OK, exactly 30 RMB. I will write you a receipt.

艾美丽： 好！
OK.

开完收据 • The repairman writes the receipt

维修员： 你保存好，这是收据，凭收据可以保修三个月。
You should keep this safe. This is a receipt. With this receipt you can guarantee repairs for 3 months.

艾美丽： 您说的是什么意思？
What does what you just said mean?

维修员：保修三个月的意思是，三个月以内坏了，我们可以免费帮你修。
"Guarantee repairs for 3 months" means if it breaks again within 3 months, we can repair it again for free.

艾美丽：哦，明白了。师傅，好像我的空调也出问题了，您能帮我看一下儿吗？
Oh, I understand. Shifu, it seems my air-conditioner has also developed a problem. Can you look at it?

维修员：对不起，修空调需要专业人士。你可以给空调的生产厂家打电话，保修卡上一般都有售后服务电话。
I'm sorry. To fix an air conditioner, you need a specialist. You can give the air conditioner's manufacturer a telephone call. The warranty card usually has a service number on it.

艾美丽：那我找一下儿，再打个电话试一试。
Then, I'll look for it, then call and try.

维修员：好的，再有问题可以给管理处打电话。
OK, if you have any more problems, you can give the management office a telephone call.

艾美丽：好的。谢谢！
OK. Thanks.

二、根据课文回答问题 • ANSWER THE FOLLOWING QUESTIONS ACCORDING TO THE TEXT

1. 艾美丽房间的什么坏了？有什么问题？
   _____

2. 维修员怎么修的？
   _____

3. 维修员为什么请艾美丽保存好收据？
   _____

4. 维修员给艾美丽修空调了吗？为什么？
   _____

5. 什么地方有售后服务电话？
   _____

三、生词 • Vocabulary

1	水龙头	shuǐlóngtóu	名	faucet, tap
2	管理	guǎnlǐ	动	to manage, to administrate
3	处	chù	名	office, place
4	管理处	guǎnlǐchù		management office
5	总是	zǒngshì	副	always
6	漏	lòu	动	to leak
7	帮	bāng	动	to help
8	马上	mǎshàng	副	immediately, right away
9	派	pài	动	to dispatch
10	维修	wéixiū	动	to maintain
11	敲	qiāo	动	to knock
12	检查	jiǎnchá	动、名	to check; inspection
13	该……了	gāi……le		[see Word Usage]
14	修理费	xiūlǐfèi		repair fee
15	一共	yígòng	副	altogether, in total
16	数	shǔ	动	to count
17	正好	zhènghǎo	副	exactly
18	开	kāi	动	to write, to give
19	收据	shōujù	名	receipt
20	保存	bǎocún	动	to keep
21	凭	píng	介、动	with, according to; to prove
22	保修	bǎoxiū		free repairs within a given period
23	……以内	……yǐnèi		within
24	免费	miǎnfèi		free, without cost
25	出	chū	动	to happen, to develop
26	对不起	duìbuqǐ		"Excuse me" "Sorry"
27	专业	zhuānyè	名	specialized line of work
28	生产	shēngchǎn	动	to produce
29	厂家	chǎngjiā	名	manufacturer
30	售	shòu	动	to sell

四、词语解释 • Word Usage

（一）、该……了

"该……了"的意思是表示某种情况应该如此或很快应该出现。句中的内容通常是即将或在未来某个时间应该发生的事情。没有否定形式。

The pattern "该…了" indicates that an action should be started immediately or that a situation should occur immediately. The sentence often indicates that a situation should occur at a specified time in the future. There is no negative form of this pattern.

例如： 1. 十二点了，该下课了。
2. 天气热了，该穿短袖衣服了。
3. 该吃饭了，我们走吧。

我们来造句 • Make your own sentence

_____

（二）、……以内

汉语中，常用"……以内"表示时间、处所、数量等的范围。"以内"不能单独使用，通常出现在名词或数量词后面。

以内 is usually used to indicate a limit for times, locations, quantities or scopes. It usually appears after nouns or quantities.

例如： 1. 两天以内我一定把事情做完。
2. 我每月吃饭的钱在1000元以内。
3. 学校以内不准骑摩托车。

我们来造句 • Make your own sentence

_____

（三）、好的，正好30块

汉语中，"正好"常用来表示时间、数量或某种情况、条件与应该的或需要的时间、数量、情况、条件相符合。也常表示巧合的意思。

正好 usually indicates that a time, quantity, or situation satisfies a requirement. It can also indicate a coincidence, as 巧合 does.

例如： 1. 这件衣服你穿正好，我穿有点儿大。
2. 他今年正好五十岁。
3. 我要去找小王，正好在图书馆碰到他。

我们来造句 • Make your own sentence

_____

○ 辨析： Distinguish between the following words

☞ "维修"和"修理"

"维修"是维护和修理的意思，是维持和保护东西原有的功能或质量，比如汽车到一定时间要进行保养，可能要进行清洗或更换一些零件，但这不一定是因为汽车坏了。而"修理"没有维护的意思，要修理的东西一定是已经坏了或有问题的东西。

维修 indicates both maintenance and repairs meant to preserve the original function or quality of an item. For example, cars need parts cleaned or changed at specific times, not because the car is broken, but to preserve its functionality. 修理, on the other hand, indicates repairs only, not maintenance. It is only used when discussing items that are already broken.

☛ "保修"和"报修"

"保修"是保证、一定可以免费修理的意思,也可以说"包修"。例如:本洗衣机三年之内保修,终身维修。意思是洗衣机在三年之内生产厂家可以免费为顾客维护或修理,三年以后还可以为顾客维护或修理,但要收费。"报修"是报告、告诉有关人员或部门什么东西坏了,请他们来修的意思。例如:"我的热水器坏了,我昨天已经报修了,但还没人来修理。"

保修, also written 包修, is a guarantee for repairs. For example, "本洗衣机三年之内保修,终身维修" guarantees customers that, within 3 years of buying a washing machine, any needed repairs are free of charge. Of course, after 3 years customers must pay for any repairs. 报修, on the other hand, is simply applying for repairs. Example: 我的热水器坏了,我昨天已经报修了,但还没人来修理。

五、汉语知识 • CHINESE KNOWLEDGE

汉语中可能或不可能的表达 • Expressing possibility

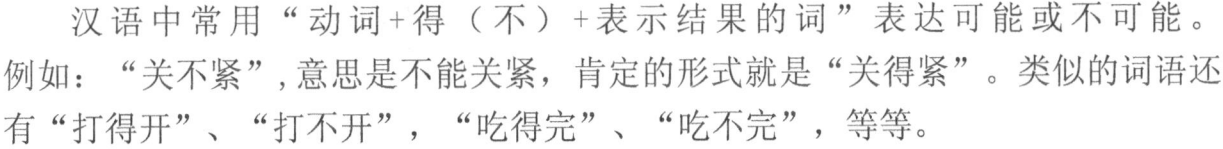

汉语中常用"动词+得(不)+表示结果的词"表达可能或不可能。例如:"关不紧",意思是不能关紧,肯定的形式就是"关得紧"。类似的词语还有"打得开"、"打不开","吃得完"、"吃不完",等等。

The pattern "verb+得+complement" is frequently used in Chinese to indicate outcomes or possibilities. The negative form is "verb+不+complement." For example, 关不紧 indicates that it is impossible to close something tightly or turn something off completely. 关得紧, meanwhile, indicates that something can be closed tightly. Similar terms include 打得开, 打不开, 吃得完, and 吃不完.

例如:
1. 米饭太多了,我吃不完。
2. 时间太短了,你做得完吗?
3. 字太小了,我看不见。
4. 这件衣服太瘦了,我穿不了。

六、相关链接 • Related Terms: household items & problems

（一）、设施报修有关的词语 • Words related to household items and problems

1	报修	bàoxiū	to apply for repairs
2	天花板	tiānhuābǎn	ceiling
3	喷头	pēntóu	shower head
4	马桶	mǎtǒng	toilet (Western-style)
5	门锁	ménsuǒ	door lock
6	柜子	guìzi	cupboard, cabinet
7	冰箱	bīngxiāng	refrigerator
8	制冷	zhìlěng	to cool, to make cold
9	热水器	rèshuǐqì	water heater
10	打不着	dǎbuzháo	can't ignite, can't light
11	图像	túxiàng	picture (as of a TV)
12	上网	shàng//wǎng	to go online
13	清楚	qīngchu	clear
14	钥匙	yàoshi	key
15	丢	diū	to lose
16	下水道	xiàshuǐdào	sewer, drainage system
17	堵	dǔ	to block, to clog

（二）、家用电器经常出的问题 • Problems with household appliances

1. 空调、冰箱不制冷了 The air-conditioner/refrigerator does not cool.
2. 热水器打不着了。 The water heater won't ignite.
3. 网络不能上网了。 I can't connect to the Internet.
4. 电视机图像不清楚了，没有声音了。 The television's picture is not clear, and there is no sound.
5. 洗衣机不能洗衣服了。 The washing machine does not work.

七、文化生活小贴士 • Cultural Tips: receipts & use of "马上"

（一）、购买商品后要索要并保留好电脑小票或发票，以便出现问题时退换。请人维修也要索要并保留好收据或发票，如在维修的保修期以内再出现问题，也应该是免费维修的。

After buying something, you should be sure to save any paper or electronic receipts. Should anything go wrong with a purchased item, a receipt is required for returns or exchanges. Whenever you have something repaired, you should be sure to ask for a receipt, as most receipts can guarantee free repairs within a certain time period.

（二）、"马上"有多快？

汉语中，"马上"、这个词常让外国朋友非常困惑。通常"马上"是表示很快、时间很短的意思，但不同的人在不同的时候对时间的理解和感觉也不一样。"马上"有时候是十分钟，也有时是一个小时。所以，有时一个人说"我一会儿就来"、"我马上就到"，但很长时间也没到。当然也有的时候是一些人故意说"马上"，以便安慰或稳住对方，所以我们要具体问题具体分析。

"马上"有多快？ can be translated as "How soon is 马上?". The term 马上 often causes frustration for foreigners. It often indicates something will be done quickly or in a short time. However, different people may have very different understandings of what "quickly" or "in a short time" mean. Sometimes 马上 may indicate ten minutes, while sometimes it may indicate an hour. So it is possible that someone will say, "我马上就到," then not arrive for a remarkably long time.

Additionally, people may only say 马上 to make someone else happy. Therefore, it is best to ask specific questions about specific times.

八、练习 • EXERCISES

（一）、填上合适的词语 • Fill in the blanks with appropriate words

帮_____、_____   漏_____、_____

数_____、_____   敲_____、_____

检查_____、_____   保存_____、_____

生产_____   专业_____   售后_____

（二）、选词填空 • Fill in the blanks with the words provided

▶ 检查   保存   意思   正好   总是   马上

1. 电视修好了，请您_____一下儿。
2. _____一千元,您数一下儿。
3. 你别着急，车_____就到了。
4. 他_____一个人看书，从不跟大家在一起。
5. 我不明白你的_____。
6. 请_____好收据，保修要凭收据的。

▶ 维修   保修   报修

1. 这台空调还在_____时间内，你为什么收_____费？
2. _____工人已经回家了，我们明天再派人去好吗？
3. 电视机已经坏了好几天了，但他还没去_____。
4. 手机一般只_____半年。

（三）、用所给词语完成句子 • Fill in the blanks with sentences using the words given in parentheses

1. A：已经十一点五十分了。
   B：_____。（该……了）

2. A：你什么时候能修完？
   B：_____。（……以内）

3. A：你在哪儿呢？什么时候到？
   B：_____。（马上）

4. A：你为什么要去南方？
   B：_____。（派）

5. A：谁都可以进校门吗？
   B：_____。（凭）

（四）、用"动词+得（不）+表示结果的词"的形式改写句子

Rewrite the following sentences using the pattern "verb+得+complement" or "verb+不+complement"

1. 人太多了，不能上车。
   _____

2. 汉语不难，能学会。
   _____

3. 饭太多了，不能吃完。
   _____

4. 字太小，不能看见。
   _____

5. 老师说的话不能听懂。
   _____

（五）、解释下面句中"意思"的意思或用法

Explain the meaning of 意思 in the following sentences

1. 汉语很难，但很有**意思**。
2. 不好**意思**，我记错了。
3. 真没**意思**！我走了。

4．我也不知道这句话是什么**意思**，你问老师吧。

（六）、词语连线 • Match words to form short phrases

派　凭　数　漏　免　敲

费　钱　门　票　水　人

（七）、用所学词语表达 • Make new sentences using the expressions below

▶ 该……了

1．八点半上课，现在八点二十九分。
2．没有现金了。
3．天气热了。
4．天气冷了。

▶ ……以内

1．如果比300元少就买。
2．不到一分钟写了65个字。
3．坐出租车不到3公里12.5元。
4．最多去三个人。

（八）、请你根据提示内容进行会话练习 • Make dialogues according to the suggestions

1．你的热水器打不着了。
2．你的空调不制冷了。
3．你的钥匙忘在房间里了。
4．你洗手间的下水道堵了。

（九）、来聊天吧 • Discuss

1．讲一段你修东西的故事。

Tell a story about fixing something or getting something fixed.

2．你觉得东西坏了，是修理好还是买新的好？为什么？

When things break, do you think it's better to fix them or buy new ones? Why?

3．在你的国家，如果买的东西坏了，应该找谁？

In your home country, when something breaks, whom should you look for or contact?

第六课 / LESSON 6

你要什么新发型?
WHAT NEW HAIRSTYLE DO YOU WANT?

这一课我们将学到 • In this lesson we will study the following:
1. 与美发有关的内容
2. 重点词语:让、正……呢、看起来
3. 辨析:"刚才"和"刚"、"最"和"更"
4. 汉语知识:(1) 汉语中的俗语
　　　　　　(2) "起来"的意义和用法

一、课文 • Text

(艾美丽和吴帅在文山湖边 • Emily and Wu Shuai are beside Wenshan Lake)

艾美丽: 刚才我约了朋友一起去美发店做头发,你要一起去吗?
Just now I made a date with a friend to got to a hair salon and get our hair done. Do you want to go together?

吴帅: 听说深大的学生凭学生证可以优惠。可我刚剪完头发,就不去了。你们去吧,你的头发是该修修了。
I hear Shenzhen University students can get special treatment with a student card. But I just cut my hair, so I won't go, OK? Your hair does need some work.

艾美丽: 我想去烫一下儿,顺便染点儿颜色,你说我染什么颜色好啊?
I want to perm my hair and, while I'm there, get it colored. You tell me, what color would look good on me?

吴帅: 你皮肤那么白,染什么颜色都好看。
With your skin that white, any color will be attractive.

艾美丽: 这叫"情人眼里出西施"。不过,我头发都开叉了,也想去保养保养。
This is called "In a lover's eyes appears Xi Shi." However, my hair's already getting split ends. Also, I want to keep my hair healthy.

吴帅: 说真的,我很喜欢你留长头发的样子。
To be serious, I really like your long-hair look.

艾美丽: 是吗?希望新发型不会让你失望。
You do? I hope my new style won't disappoint you.

在美发店 • In a hair salon

 理发师: 小姐，该你了，请这边来。
Miss, it's your turn. Please come this way.

 艾美丽: 好的。
OK.

 理发师: 我们先洗（一）下儿头。请问你要什么洗发水？
First, we'll wash your hair. May I ask what shampoo you want?

 艾美丽: 就要普通的就行了。
Just the regular one is fine.

 理发师: 噢，这边请。请问你要什么新发型？
Oh. This way please. May I ask, what new hairstyle do you want?

 艾美丽: 我就是想剪短一点儿。
I just want my hair cut a bit shorter.

 理发师: 你的头发都开叉了，做个焗油吧，我们有一批新产品，顾客做了效果很好。
Your hair has split ends. We could do a hot oil treatment. We have a line of new products. Our customers have all had good results.

 艾美丽: 我正想做个保养呢。
I do want to keep my hair healthy.

 理发师: 那我们先焗油，然后再剪。
Then, we'll first do a hot oil treatment, and then cut your hair.

 艾美丽: 好的。
OK.

剪完发以后 • After Emily's hair has been cut

 理发师: 你看，这样可以吗？
Look, is this way OK?

 维修员: 我想前面再剪短一点儿。
I want the front cut a bit shorter.

 理发师: 好了。嗯，这样看起来更精神一点儿了。我帮你吹一下儿吧。
OK. Oh, this way looks a bit sassier. I'll blow-dry your hair.

 维修员: 嗯，好吧。
Umm, OK.

 理发师： 你看这样满意吗？你照照镜子。
Look. Is this satisfactory? You can check in the mirror.

 维修员： 嗯，挺好的，谢谢。
Umm, quite good. Thanks.

二、根据课文回答问题 • Answer the following questions according to the text

1. 吴帅觉得艾美丽染什么颜色头发好看？
   _____

2. 艾美丽为什么想去保养保养？
   _____

3. 吴帅喜欢艾美丽留什么发型？
   _____

4. 艾美丽要的什么洗发水？
   _____

5. 头发剪短以后怎么样？
   _____

三、生词 • Vocabulary

1	发型	fàxíng	名	hair style
2	刚才	gāngcái	名	shortly, the recent past
3	美发	měifà		to have one's hair styled
4	美发店	měifàdiàn	名	hair salon
5	头发	tóufa	名	hair
6	优惠	yōuhuì	动、形	to receive special treatment
7	刚	gāng	副	shortly
8	剪	jiǎn	动	to cut
9	烫	tàng	动	to perm hair, to curl hair
10	顺便	shùnbiàn	副	on the way, at one's convenience
11	染	rǎn	动	to color, to dye
12	皮肤	pífū	名	skin
13	情人	qíngrén	名	beloved, lover
14	眼（眼睛）	yǎn(yǎnjing)	名	eye

15	开	kāi	动	to open
16	叉	chà	名	fork
17	开叉	kāichà		split ends
18	保养	bǎoyǎng	动、名	to keep in good condition or good health
19	留	liú	动	to grow
20	样子	yàngzi	名	style, shape, appearance
21	失望	shīwàng	形	disappointed
22	头	tóu	名	head
23	洗发水	xǐfàshuǐ	名	shampoo
24	普通	pǔtōng	形	normal
25	噢	ō	叹	[an exclamation: Oh!]
26	短	duǎn	形	short
27	焗	jú	动	hot
28	油	yóu	名	oil
29	焗油	júyóu		hot oil
30	批	pī	量	line, group, batch
31	产品	chǎnpǐn	名	product
32	顾客	gùkè	名	customer
33	效果	xiàoguǒ	名	effect, outcome
34	正	zhèng	副	just
35	起来	qǐlái		to rise, to get up
36	看起来	kànqǐlái		to look like, to look as though
37	更	gèng	副	more
38	精神	jīngshen	形、名	spirited, sassy; spirit, energy
39	吹	chuī	动	to blow (dry)
40	满意	mǎnyì	形	satisfactory, satisfied
41	照	zhào	动	to look, to check

专名词 • Proper Names

42	文山湖	wénshānhú		Wenshan Lake
43	西施	xīshī		Xi Shi, one of the Four Beauties of ancient China

四、词语解释 • Word Usage

（一）、希望新发型不会<u>让</u>你<u>失望</u>

在这里，"让"的意思是"使"、"致使"的意思。常用的句式是"A让B……"。在句中，"A"、"B"可以是事物，也可以是人，"A"是"让"的主体，"B"既是"让"的宾语，同时也是产生变化或结果的主体。在"希望新发型不会让你失望。"这个句子中，"新发型"是A，"你"是B，"失望"是结果。

Here, 让 has the same meaning as 使 and can be understood as "cause" or "make." In the commonly used pattern "A让B…," A is the subject of the overall sentence, and 让 is a verb, while B acts as both the direct object of 让 and the subject of a following clause. In the sentence "希望新发型不会让你失望," 新发型 (A) is the subject of the larger sentence, and 你 (B) is both the direct object of 让, as well as the acting subject in the clause "你失望."

例如： 1. 这件事让大家很高兴。
2. 这样的天气让我感觉很不舒服。
3. 你太让我失望了。

我们来造句 • Make your own sentence

_____

（二）、正……呢

汉语中，"正……呢"常用来表示动作、行为、事件的持续状态，也可表示不同的事件、动作、行为正好在同时发生。句中通常不能出现表示完成或结果的词语。也可用"在……呢"、"正在……呢"表示。

The pattern "正…呢" is often used to indicate that an action or situation is currently happening or ongoing. It can also indicate that an action or situation was happening at a given point in time. "在…呢" and "正在…呢" can be used in the same way.

例如： 1. 老师正上课呢。
2. 小王在打电话呢。
3. 我去找他时，他正在吃饭呢。

我们来造句 • Make your own sentence

_____

（三）、看起来

在这里，"看起来"表示估计、推测、打量的意思。常用来表达人的主观感觉或判断。常作插入语或出现在句子的前一部分。

Here, "看起来" indicates a guess, supposition, or conjecture. It is most often used to express personal judgments and is often used at the beginning of a sentence or as a parenthetical expression.

例如： 1. 她看起来只有三十岁。
2. 看起来，天要下雨了，我们快走吧。

我们来造句 • Make your own sentence

_____

课文注释：Key Points in the Text

☞ 情人眼里出西施

"情人眼里出西施"的意思是，如果两人是情人，无论一方是什么样子，另一方都会觉得很漂亮。"西施"是中国古代非常有名的四大美人之一。

"In a lover's eyes appears Xi Shi" means that, when two people are in love, it doesn't matter how they actually look. Each will always think the other is attractive. Xi Shi was one of the Four Beauties of ancient China.

○ 辨析：Distinguish between the following words

☛ "刚才" 和 "刚"

"刚才" 和 "刚" 都含有时间短的意思，但又有很多不同的地方。

"刚才" 是一个表示时间的名词，它的意思是指在说话前不久的时间。而 "刚" 是副词，是表示某事发生的时间距说话人说话的时间很近。它只能用在动词前。"刚才" 常用来表示变化与 "现在" 对比出现。

刚才 and 刚 both indicate a short time. However, 刚才 can function as a noun, in which usage it indicates the recent past or a time just prior to the sentence. 刚, on the other hand, is an adverb. It must be used with another verb and can be used to discuss events in either the recent or distant past.

例如：1. 我刚到学校。
2. 刚下完雨，地上还有很多水。
3. 刚才下雨了，现在停了。
4. 刚才我去图书馆了。
5. 刚才他还在哭，现在却笑了。

☛ "最" 和 "更"

"最" 和 "更" 都含有比较和程度高的意思，但两者又有区别。

"最" 表示超过所有比较的对象，但并不考虑比较对象原有的程度如何。而 "更" 则表示在原有程度上的加强和提高。"更" 常常出现在比较句中，有比较的对象。"最" 通常不会出现在比较句中，没有具体的比较对象。

最 and 更 both indicate a relatively high degree. However, 最 indicates a degree that cannot be exceeded and does so without making a clear comparison. 更, on the other hand, does make a clear comparison and is used in comparative sentences.

例如：1. 他是我们班汉语水平最高的。
2. 我觉得汉语的发音最难。
3. 汉语的发音很难，但汉字更难。
（意思是：承认发音很难，认为汉字比发音难）
4. 他比我更喜欢打太极拳。
（意思是：我也喜欢打太极拳，但他比我喜欢）

五、汉语知识 • Chinese Knowledge

（一）、汉语中的俗语 • Common Sayings

汉语中，有一些词语独立成句，表达一个完整的意思，经过长时间的广泛的传诵，成为社会大众掌握和使用的话语，人们称为"俗语"、"俗话"。课文中的"情人眼里出西施"就是这样的俗语。

Some expressions or phrases can stand alone as sentences. Over long periods of time and through continual repetition, some such expressions become a part of common conversation. They eventually can be used to express a complete idea in relatively few words. Such expressions are called 俗语 or 俗话, or common sayings. "情人眼里出西施," for example, is a 俗语.

（二）、"起来"的意义和用法 • The meaning and usage of "起来"

汉语中，"起来"有很多种意思，可以跟许多动词、形容词一起使用。如果动词带宾语或是动宾结构的，就要把宾语放在"起"和"来"之间。主要用法有：

起来 has many meanings and uses. It can be used with adjectives and verbs. When used with a verb that has a direct object, 起来 should be placed between verb and object. Important uses include the following:

▶ 1. 表示起身的意思 • Indicating awakening

　　例如：1. 我今天5点就起来看书了。
　　　　　2. 他已经起来了，别叫他了。

▶ 2. 表示由下向上的意思，出现在动词后

Indicating movement from a lower to a higher place, used after verbs

　　例如：1. 他从椅子上站起来，走了出去。
　　　　　2. 我们把桌子抬起来吧。

▶ 3. 表示动作完成或产生某种结果的意思

Indicating an action has been completed or produced a result

　　例如：1. 我想起来了。
　　　　　2. 我把书收起来了。

▶ 4. 表示动作、状态开始并继续进行下去。

Indicating the beginning or continuation of an action or a situation

　　例如：1. 刚才还是晴天，可现在下起雨来了。
　　　　　　（表示状态开始并进行下去，带宾语）
　　　　　2. 老师说完后，大家就开始做了起来。
　　　　　3. 夏天到了，天气热起来了。

▶ 5. 与动词一起用，表示关注、做某事或对某种情况、现象的估计或推测，一般出现在句子的前一部分或作插入语，而后面句子的内容则是关注和做了某事的结果

以及对情况、现象的估计或推测后得出的结论。有时也可省略为"起"。

When used after verbs, it can indicate a personal judgment regarding an action or a situation. It is usually used at the beginning of a clause or as a parenthetical expression. In such cases, 起 can be omitted.

例如： 1. 这种水果看起来不好看，但吃起来很好吃。
　　　 2. 看起来，今天要下雨。
　　　 3. 说起这件事来，大家都很高兴。
　　　 4. 说起王老师，大家都说他是好老师。

六、相关链接，与理发有关的词语 • Related Terms: beauty salons

1	美容美发厅	měiróngměifàtīng	beauty salon
2	化妆品	huàzhuāngpǐn	cosmetics, make up
3	脸型	liǎnxíng	facial shape
4	预约	yùyuē	to make an appointment

七、文化生活小贴士 • Tips for Daily Life: "洗头"

关于"洗头"

广东的理发店，"洗头"是一个服务项目，不同于一般的洗头，而是包含着头部及全身的按摩，"洗头"的方式也有很多种，比如"泰式"、"中式"等，顾客还可以在"洗头"项目中选择洗脸、洗耳朵等服务。

In hair salons in Guangdong, 洗头 is a commonly offered service. It does not necessarily mean simply washing hair. Rather, it may also include a scalp massage or even a full body massage. A variety of 洗头 styles are offered, including "Thai" and "Chinese" styles. Clients can also choose to have their faces or ears cleaned, along with other services.

八、练习 • Exercises

（一）、填上合适的词语 • Fill in the blanks with appropriate words

_____、____边　　_____、____店

洗_____、_____　　更_____、_____

顾客_____　　效果_____　　保养_____

（二）、选词填空 • Fill in the blanks with the words provided

▶ 顺便　失望　普通　满意　精神　优惠　样子　产品

1. 这个厂家生产的_____很好。
2. 中介公司的服务让租客很_____。
3. 老师很_____同学们的考试。
4. 我去超市，可以_____帮你买咖啡。
5. 小张最近瘦了，看上去比以前更_____了。
6. 茂业百货正打折呢，现在买化妆品很_____。
7. 这个菜很_____，我也会做。
8. 这台空调的_____很漂亮，可是有点儿贵。

▶ 刚　　刚才

1. 我们_____来，你怎么就要走啊？
2. 我_____在超市买了一些水果。
3. _____小王把这件事告诉我了。
4. _____还是晴天，现在怎么下雨了？

▶ 最　　更

1. 他是我们班汉语_____好的。
2. 听说明天的考试比今天的_____难。
3. 我_____喜欢吃四川菜。
4. 我觉得你留长发比留短发_____漂亮。

（三）、用所给词语完成句子 • Fill in the blanks with sentences using the words given in parentheses

1. A：你去找他的时候他在做什么呢？
   B：_____。（正……呢）
2. A：你去哪儿了？
   B：_____。（刚）
3. A：王老师已经五十多岁了。
   B：_____。（看起来）
4. A：我的冰箱不制冷了。
   B：_____。（让）
5. A：你看我穿这条裙子怎么样？
   B：_____。（更）

（四）、词语连线 • Match words to form short phrases

皮肤　　头发　　留　　照　　染

镜子　　短发　　颜色　　开叉　　白

（五）、做游戏 • Play a game

分小组竞赛。女生做顾客，男生当理发师。女生选择一个自己喜欢的发型，跟你的理发师用普通话沟通，最后，理发师要把女生跟她表述的发型画出来，最接近者为赢。

Divide into groups. Women play customers. Men play hair stylists. Women choose their favorite hair styles and try to describe them to their hair stylists. Men draw the hair styles described as best as they can. The hairstylist whose drawing most resembles his customer's selected hair style wins.

（六）、连连看，判断动词能否跟"头发"搭配，能的话，请造句。

Decide which of the following verbs can be used before 头发. Make a sentence for each verb that can.

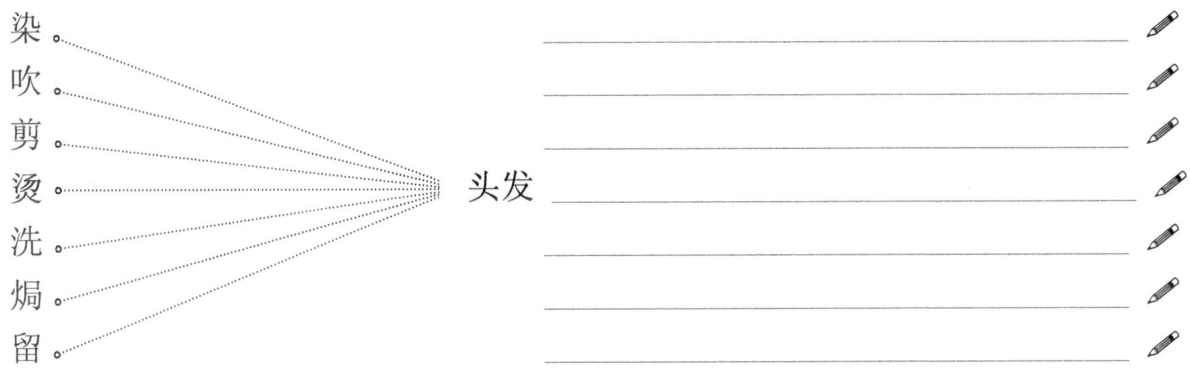

（七）、说说写写 • Speak and Write

1. 说出跟头发有关的动词或理发店的服务项目名称并试着写一写。

   Say any words you know related to hairstyles or hair salons. Then try to write them.

2. 说出跟头发有关的日用品名称并试着写一写。

   Say what hair products you know. Then try and write them.

（八）、描述一位同学的发型，请全班同学猜一猜说的是谁？

Describe a classmate's hairstyle. The class tries to guess who is being described.

（九）、来聊天吧 • Discuss

1. 你留过什么样的发型，你最喜欢什么发型？为什么？

   What kind of hairstyles have you had? What is your favorite hairstyle? Why?

2. 你觉得发型对一个人重要吗？为什么？

   Do you think a person's hairstyle is important? If so, why?

第七课 / LESSON 7
我们去听音乐会吧
WE CAN GO LISTEN TO A CONCERT, OK?

这一课我们将学到 • In this lesson we will study the following:
1. 与约会有关的内容
2. 重点词语：对了、别提了、你怎么这么晚才到、我六点就出门了、也是
3. 辨析："才"和"就"、
4. 汉语知识："动词+个+宾语"的意义和用法

一、课文 • Text

（艾美丽和吴帅在校园 • Emily and Wu Shuai are on campus）

 吴帅： 你星期六下午有时间吗？
On Saturday afternoon, do you have time?

 艾美丽： 有啊。你有什么事？
I do. You have something to do?

 吴帅： 你猜。
You guess.

 艾美丽： 我猜不着。
I can't guess.

 吴帅： 那天是七夕，中国的情人节。
That day is Qixi, China's Sweethearts' Day.

 艾美丽： 哦，对了，我忘了。你打算怎么过？
Oh, that's right. I forgot. How do you plan to spend it?

 吴帅： 我们去听音乐会吧。
We can go listen to a concert, OK?

艾美丽： 好主意！我正想去听音乐会呢，你真了解我。不过，我们现在去买票还来得及吗？
Good idea. I did want to go listen to a concert. You really understand me. But, if we go to buy tickets now, is there still time?

吴帅： （吴帅掏出票）你看，这是什么？票早就订好了。
(Wu Shuai takes out two tickets) Look. What are these? I've already bought tickets.

艾美丽： 太好了！在哪儿？几点的？
Great! Where is it? What time?

吴帅： 在深圳音乐厅，八点开始。是一场钢琴独奏音乐会。
It's at the Shenzhen Music Hall. It starts at 8 o'clock. It's a piano solo concert.

艾美丽： 那我们先一起吃个饭，然后再去听音乐。
Then, first we can have dinner together, and then go to the concert.

吴帅： 好的，那我们六点半在地铁站见。
OK. Then let's meet at 6:30 at the metro station.

艾美丽： 好，不见不散。
OK. If you don't see me, don't walk off.

在地铁站 • At the metro station

吴帅： 不好意思，我迟到了。你等了很久了吧？
Sorry. I arrived late. You waited a very long time, right?

艾美丽： 等了一会儿。都七点了，你怎么这么晚才到？
I waited a while. It's already 7. How can you arrive this late?

吴帅： 别提了，我六点就出门了，路上塞车太严重了。
Don't talk about it. At 6 o'clock, I left home. The traffic on the way was too heavy.

艾美丽： 也是，正好是下班高峰期，塞车很正常。我们走吧。
Yeah, just now is the after-work rush hour. Busy traffic is normal. Let's go.

吴帅： 怎么，生气了？（吴帅拿出玫瑰花）请艾美丽小姐原谅我吧！
What? Are you angry? (Wu Shuai takes out a bouquet of roses.) Please, Miss Emily, forgive me.

艾美丽： 谁生气了？我只是担心嘛。
Who's angry? I'm just worried.

二、根据课文回答问题 • Answer the following questions according to the text

1. "七夕"是什么节日?
   _____

2. 吴帅和艾美丽"七夕"怎么过的?
   _____

3. 吴帅和艾美丽约好在哪儿见面?
   _____

4. 吴帅为什么迟到了?
   _____

5. 艾美丽生气了吗?
   _____

三、生词 • Vocabulary

1	音乐	yīnyuè	名	music
2	音乐会	yīnyuèhuì	名	concert
3	猜	cāi	动	to guess
4	着	zháo	动	to reach a goal
5	猜不着	cāibuzháo		to be unable to guess
6	节	jié	名	festival, holiday
7	忘	wàng	动	to forget
8	打算	dǎsuan	动、名	to plan for; plan
9	主意	zhǔyì	名	idea
10	来得及	láidejí		not too late, still in time
11	掏	tāo	动	to take out, to withdraw
12	早	zǎo	形	early
13	开始	kāishǐ	动、名	to begin; beginning
14	场	chǎng	量	[a measure word for activities]
15	独奏	dúzòu		solo
16	音乐厅	yīnyuètīng	名	music hall
17	不见不散	bújiànbúsàn		[often said after making plans for meeting, literally "No see, no disperse]

18	迟到	chídào		to be late
19	晚	wǎn	形	late
20	提	tí	动	to bring up, to mention
21	别提了	biétíle		"Don't bring up…"
22	路上	lùshang		on the road, on the way
23	塞	sāi	动	to fill, to block
24	严重	yánzhòng	形	serious, critical
25	（下）班	(xià)bān	名	(finish) work
26	高峰	gāofēng	名	top, peak
27	期	qī	名	time, period
28	高峰期	gāofēngqī		rush hour
29	正常	zhèngcháng	形	normal
30	生气	shēng//qì	（动宾）动	to become angry
31	玫瑰	méiguī	名	rose
32	花	huār	名	flower
33	原谅	yuánliàng	动	to forgive
34	担心	dānxīn	动	to worry
35	嘛	ma	助	[a particle, suggests something is obvious]

专名词 • Proper Names

36	七夕	qīxī		7th evening of the 7th lunar month

四、词语解释 • Word Usage

（一）、<u>对了</u>，我忘了

在这里，"对了"表示突然想起什么事来的意思。常作插入语。

Here, 对了 indicates the speaker has suddenly remembered something. It is most often a parenthetical expression.

例如：1. 对了，我该去汉语角练汉语了。
2. 对了，我忘了给妈妈打电话。

我们来造句 • Make your own sentence

_____

（二）、别提了

在这里，"提"的意思是"谈起""说起"。"别提了"就是"不要说了"，表示不愿意、不想谈到的意思。常作插入语。有时也表示程度高或夸张的语气，常用格式为"别提多……了"。

Here, 提 means to start a discussion or raise a point about something. 别提了, then, means the same as 不要说了. It indicates the speaker is unwilling to or doesn't wish to discuss a specific topic. It is often a parenthetical expression. When written 别提多…了, it is emphatic.

例如： 1. 别提了，今天的考试太难了，我都不会做。
2. 别提了，我把钥匙忘在房间了。
3. 今天天气别提多热了。（意思是：天气很热）
4. 他的汉语别提多好了。（意思是：他的汉语很好）

我们来造句 • Make your own sentence

_____

（三）、你怎么这么晚**才**到？

在这里，"才"出现在动词前，表示说话人认为、觉得动作发生或结束的时间晚、时间长、不容易、不顺利等。常用来表达说话人的主观感觉。

When placed before a verb, 才 indicates that an action is performed later, takes a longer time, is harder, or is more complex than the speaker would expect. It is used to express personal opinions.

例如： 1. 我找了他三次才找到。
2. 你怎么才吃饭，都几点了？
3. 他下个月才回国。

我们来造句 • Make your own sentence

_____

（四）、我六点**就**出门了

在这里，"就"出现在动词前，表示说话人认为动作发生的时间早、时间短、容易、顺利等。常用来表达说话人的主观感觉。

When placed before a verb, 就 indicates that an action is performed earlier, takes less time, or is easier than the speaker would expect. It is used to express personal opinions.

例如： 1. 我们两天前就到了。
2. 他明天就回国了。

我们来造句 • Make your own sentence

_____

（五）、**也是**，现在是下班高峰期

在这里，"也是"的意思是表示同意对方说的话或承认某个事实。通常出现在答话中或作插入语。

Here, 也是 indicates agreement with what someone else has said or acceptance of a situation. It is often used as a response or as a parenthetical expression.

例如：1. A：我说的话他听不懂。
　　　　B：也是，他太小了，怎么能明白你说的话。
　　　2. A：我们还是做公交车去吧。
　　　　B：也是，坐出租车太贵了，我们坐公交车去吧。

我们来造句 • Make your own sentence

_____

○ 辨析：Distinguish between the following words

☞ "才" 和 "就"

"才"表示说话人认为动作发生的时间晚、时间长、不容易、不顺利等，"就"表示说话人认为动作发生的时间早、时间短、容易、顺利等。在这些意义上，它们是一对意思相反的词。但它们都是表示说话人的主观评价，说话人的感觉，与客观事实无关。比如：1. 我六点就到图书馆等你了。2. 我六点才到图书馆。同样是"六点"但说话人的感觉不同，所以一个用了"才"，一个用了"就"。

才 indicates that an action is performed later, takes a longer time, is harder, or is more complex than the speaker would expect. 就 indicates that an action is performed earlier, takes less time, or is easier than the speaker would expect. As an illustration, in both "我六点就到图书馆" and "我六点才到图书馆" the speaker arrived at the library at 6:00. However, in the first sentence, the speaker feels that 6:00 is quite early and, thus, uses 就. In the second sentence, the speaker feels that 6:00 is quite late and, thus, uses 才.

五、汉语知识 • CHINESE KNOWLEDGE

"动词+个+宾语" 的意义和用法 • The pattern "verb+个+noun," meaning and usage

"个"是汉语中常用的量词，可以和很多名词搭配。但"个"也有一些其它用法。课文中"吃个饭"中的"个"不表示数量，而是表示一种轻松、随便的语气。很多动宾关系的词或短语都可以和"个"连用，构成"动词+个+宾语"这样的格式。比如："洗个头"、"买个菜"、"看个书"、"喝个酒"等等，有时还可以两个连用，比如：他们经常在一起喝个酒、吃个饭什么的。

个 is a measure word that can be used before many nouns. In addition, 个 also has a number of other uses. In the text, the 个 in the phrase 吃个饭 does not indicate quantity. Rather it indicates a relaxed or casual tone. 个 can be put between many verb-object pairs to similar effect, as with 洗个头, 买个菜, 看个书, and 喝个酒. All indicate a relaxed tone rather than quantity. More than one "verb+个+noun" pattern can be used in one sentence. Example: 他们经常在一起喝个酒，吃个饭什么的.

例如： 1. 我太累了，想睡个觉。
　　　 2. 他平时的运动就是爬个山、打个球什么的。

六、相关链接，与娱乐、休闲有关的其他词语 • Related Terms: entertainment

1	电影	diànyǐng	film
2	电视	diànshì	TV
3	录像	lùxiàng	video recording
4	京剧	jīngjù	Beijing Opera
5	芭蕾舞	bāléiwǔ	ballet
6	文艺演出	wényì yǎnchū	art performance

七、文化生活小贴士 • Cultural Tips: China festivals & dating

（一）、七夕——中国的情人节 • The Night of Sevens—China's Sweethearts' Festival

中国的农历七月初七，有一个好听的名字——七夕。传说，牛郎出生在一户非常穷困的人家。父母去世后，哥嫂只分给他一头老牛。他虽受够了贫困与虐待之苦，但是他天性善良，不怨不恨，只与老牛相依为命。织女原是天上的仙女，她来到人间，嫁给了牛郎。王母发现后将织女和牛郎分开。后来天帝大发善心允许他们七夕这一天相会。后来人们就把这一天叫做中国的情人节。

In the Chinese lunar calendar, the 7th day of the 7th month has a pleasant sounding name—Qixi. According to legend, Niu Lang was born into a very poor family. After his parents died, his brother and sister-in-law gave him nothing but an old cow as his part of the inheritance. Although he suffered from significant poverty and cruelties, he was nonetheless naturally kind-hearted, incapable of anger or hate. He and his old cow relied on one another to survive.

Zi Nü was originally a fairy in the heavens. She came into the world of men and married Niu Lang. Once the Queen of the Fairies discovered this, she took Zi Nü back to the heavens. Sometime later, the Lord of Heaven, in an act of mercy, allowed Niu Lang and Zi Nü to meet for one day each year on the 7th day of the 7th month. Later people began calling this day "China's Sweethearts' Festival."

（二）、约会的礼仪 • The etiquette of dating

情侣、朋友之间的约会，应该遵守必要的礼节。中国人喜欢用委婉的方式表达自己的情感，要学会听中国人的言外之意。

When inviting friends or a romantic interest out, it is best to follow local customs. Chinese people generally prefer to express their feelings indirectly, so it is important not only to understand what is said, but also to understand what is left unsaid.

▶ 邀请——给对方一定的选择空间，不能强迫他人和自己约会。如果对方表现出不愿意参与，可能会说："下次有机会再约。""等你有时间我们再见面。"委婉结束这个邀请。

Invitations — When inviting people out, be sure to give them adequate freedom to choose and avoid making them feel pressured into accepting. If someone turns down an invitation, you can say, "下次有机会再约" or "等你有时间我们再见." These are indirect and polite ways to end the conversation or end the topic.

▶ 接受邀请——如果可以当场决定接受邀请，最好能爽快地答应，答应之后不要违约，准时到场。如有特殊情况，要提前通知邀请者。如果在当时无法作出决定，可以告诉对方："让我再考虑考虑。""我等会儿再给你答复。"

Accepting invitations — If you are willing to accept an invitation at the time, it's best to accept in a straightforward manner. Do not agree to meet with someone unless you are sure you have time. If you are unsure, you can say, "让我考虑考虑" or "我等会儿再给你答应." If you do accept an invitation, be sure to be on time. If unexpected circumstances will prevent you from being on time, be sure to contact the other person.

▶ 拒绝——中国人在拒绝邀请的时候，会先说很多的客观理由，最后才告诉对方自己不能接受邀请。有时候，当女生拒绝自己不感兴趣的男生的约会邀请时，可能会说"我很忙，有空再说""过两天再给你答复""等以后有机会吧"，这个时候，不能从字面含义理解她的意思了，要明白，她是不想和你见面。

Declining invitations — When declining invitations, Chinese people will often give many reasons before saying that they can't accept the invitation. When declining an invitation from a man, many women will often say something like "我很忙，有空再说," "过两天再给你回答," or "等以后有机会吧." These can best be understood as expressions that a woman has no interest in meeting or dating, though the sentences' literal meanings are different. [Note: 两天, here, is not "two days" but an indefinite time in the future.]

八、练习 • Exercises

（一）、填上合适的词语 • Fill in the blanks with appropriate words

掏_____、_____　　　　订_____、_____

开始_____、_____　　　了解_____、_____

不见_____　　　　　　　塞车_____

（二）、选词填空 • Fill in the blanks with the words provided

路上　　了解　　正常　　迟到　　严重　　主意　　生气　　原谅　　担心

1. 最近天气不太_____，前两天那么热，可今天又这么冷。

2. 他每天上课都_____，今天老师没让他进门。
3. 他还在_____，我们等他一会儿吧。
4. 现在气候问题越来越_____。
5. 我不知道怎么办好，你给我出个_____吧。
6. 我们只见过两次，所以对他不太_____。
7. 别_____，考试不难。
8. 别_____了，对不起，都是我错了。
9. 你这么做，朋友是不会_____你的。

（三）、用所给词语完成句子 • Fill in the blanks with sentences using the words given in parentheses

1. A:下课以后你做什么？
   B:_____。（打算）
2. A:听说你小提琴拉得非常好。
   B:_____？（谁）
3. A:我们去哪儿玩儿好？
   B:_____。（主意）
4. A:我们下午两点在校门口见面好吗？
   B:_____。（不见不散）
5. A:都四点半了，快走吧！
   B:_____。（来得及）
6. A:他怎么还不回来？
   B:_____。（担心）
7. A:你看上去不开心的样子。
   B:_____。（别提了）
8. A:他怎么了？
   B:_____。（生气）

（四）、用"才"和"就"填空 • Complete the sentences with 才 or 就

1. 音乐会8:30开始，我们7:00____到了。
2. 音乐会8:30开始，我们9:00____到。
3. 太极拳很难学，我学了三个月____学会。
4. 他写得很明白，我一看____懂了。
5. 他说他马上____到，可我们等了三个小时他____来。
6. 我等了他半天他____到，我都快急死了。

（五）、填反义词 • Write an antonym for each of the following words

长—— 早—— 便宜—— 好——

真—— 新—— 赔——

（六）、根据时间从早到晚排列下面一段话

Put the following sentences into chronological order

1. 晚上十二点，我在宿舍看书。
2. 我早上六点去跑步。
3. 在早上七点去买早餐。
4. 晚上七点半，我和我男朋友一起去听音乐会。
5. 中午我在家吃饭。
6. 下午四点我去超市买菜。

（七）、对话练习 • Conversation Practice

1. 假如你有一个老朋友要来深圳玩，在电话里约定你们在哪见面。

   Pretend a friend is coming to visit Shenzhen. Have a conversation agreeing on where to meet.

2. 你想约你的同学星期五下午3点去买东西，但是他没有时间，你和他重新定时间。

   You want to invite a friend to go shopping at 3 o'clock on Friday, but your friend doesn't have time. Decide together on a new time.

3. 向你的朋友推荐深圳好玩的地方、好吃的餐厅，邀请他们和你一起去。

   Tell your friend about a good entertainment venue or restaurant in Shenzhen. Invite your friend to go there together.

（八）模拟约会 • Invite your classmates

看电影场次表，约你的同学一起去看电影。

Look at the showings times below. Invite classmates to go watch a movie together.

时间	语言	放映厅	票价
13:20	英文	4厅(136座)	40元
17:15	英文	4厅(136座)	40元

（九）、来聊天吧 • Discuss

1. 和朋友讨论你的爱好，谈谈你觉得什么"有意思"，什么"没意思"。

   Discuss your hobbies. Use 有意思 and 没意思 to describe what pastimes you find interesting and uninteresting.

2. 告诉你的朋友你"听说"的事情。

   Using 听说, tell your classmates about something you've heard or learned recently.

第八课 / LESSON 8

吃哪种药好得快?
WHICH KIND OF MEDICINE WORKS FAST?

这一课我们将学到 • In this lesson we will study the following:
1. 与买药、看病有关的内容
2. 重点词语：开始……，后来……，现在……
3. 汉语知识：肯定+否定的疑问形式

一、课文 • TEXT

(艾美丽感冒了，她在一家药店买药 • Emily has caught a cold and is buying medicine in a drug store)

 售货员： 欢迎光临，请问您需要什么？
Welcome here. May I ask what you need?

 艾美丽： 我感冒了，鼻塞，嗓子不舒服，头也疼。
I've caught a cold. My nose is blocked, and my throat is not comfortable. My head also hurts.

 售货员： 你可以吃这种药，这种是中药。
You can take this kind of medicine. This kind is Chinese medicine.

 艾美丽： 那种呢？
And that kind?

 售货员： 那种药也不错，是西药。
That kind of medicine also isn't bad. It's Western medicine.

 艾美丽： 吃哪种药好得快？
Which kind of medicine works fast?

 售货员： 两种药成分不一样，效果差不多。不过，西药吃完了可能会犯困。
The two kinds of medicine, the ingredients aren't the same, but the effects aren't much different. However, once you've taken the Western medicine, it's possible you'll fan kun.

艾美丽： "犯困"是什么？
What is "fan kun?"

售货员： 就是想睡觉。
It means you'll want to sleep.

艾美丽： 哦，我明天还有考试，那我还是吃中药吧。
Oh, tomorrow I still have to take a test. So I'd better take the Chinese medicine.

售货员： 那好，我给你拿一盒。
Ok. I'll give you a box.

艾美丽： 好，这药怎么吃啊？
OK. This medicine, how do I take it?

售货员： 上面有说明：一天吃三次，一次吃两粒，饭后服用，温开水送下。
There are directions on top: Every day, take 3 times; every time, take two pills; take after eating; rinse them down with warm water.

艾美丽： 好的，谢谢！
OK. Thanks.

售货员： 不客气，请慢走！
Don't mention it. Take care.

艾美丽吃了药后还是没有好，她现在在医院看病 Emily hasn't improved after taking Chinese medicine. Now, she's seeing a doctor in a hospital

医生： 你哪里不舒服？
Where are you uncomfortable?

艾美丽： 我感冒了，有5天了，鼻塞，嗓子疼，头也疼。
I have a cold. I've had it for five days. My nose is blocked, and my throat is not comfortable. My head also hurts.

医生： 发不发烧？
Do you have a fever or not?

艾美丽： 发烧。
I do.

医生： 几度？
What is your temperature?

艾美丽： 38度。
38 degrees Celsius.

医生： 咳嗽吗？
Coughing?

艾美丽： 开始不咳嗽，后来有一点儿，现在很厉害。
When it started, I didn't have a cough. Afterwards, I had a bit of a cough. Now it's really bad.

医生： 有没有痰？
Do you have phlegm or not?

艾美丽： 没有。
I don't.

医生： 张开嘴巴，"啊"。
Open up your mouth: "Ah."

艾美丽： 啊。
Ah.

医生： 嗓子发炎了。你先去验血，然后再来找我。
Your throat shows some inflammation. First go and test your blood. Then come back and find me.

艾美丽： 好的。
OK.

艾美丽验血后回来，把化验结果给医生看 After testing her blood, Emily returns and gives the results to the doctor

医生： 你是病毒感染。我先给你开点儿药，有没有对什么药过敏？
You have a viral infection. First, I'll give you a prescription. Do you have any medicinal allergies?

艾美丽： 没有。医生，我要打针吗？
I don't. Doctor, do I need a shot?

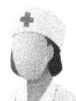
医生： 输液吧，输液比打针消炎快。
An IV, OK? Compared to a shot, IVs reduce inflammation faster.

艾美丽： 嗯，好的。
Umm, OK.

医生： 你先去交费、取药，然后再去输液。要多喝水，多休息。
First, go and pay, get your medicine, and then go get the IV. You should drink a lot of water and get a lot of rest.

艾美丽： 好的。谢谢！
OK. Thanks.

二、根据课文回答问题 • ANSWER THE FOLLOWING QUESTIONS ACCORDING TO THE TEXT

1. 艾美丽怎么了？哪儿不舒服？
   _____

2. "犯困"是什么意思？
   _____

3. 艾美丽发烧吗？多少度？
   _____

4. 艾美丽有没有对什么药过敏?

5. 医生让艾美丽回家以后做什么?

三、生词 • Vocabulary

1	药	yào	名	medicine
2	感冒	gǎnmào	动、名	to catch a cold; a cold
3	鼻	bí	名	nose
4	嗓子	sǎngzi	名	throat
5	疼	téng	形	painful, sore
6	中药	zhōngyào	名	Chinese medicine
7	西药	xīyào	名	Western medicine
8	成份	chéngfèn	名	composition, mixture of ingredients
9	犯	fàn	动	to recur, to flare up
10	困	kùn	动	to be sleepy, to be drowsy
11	犯困	fànkùn		experience drowsiness
12	睡觉	shuì//jiào	(动宾)动	to sleep
13	考试	kǎo//shì	(动宾)动	to have an exam, to take an exam
14	盒	hé	量	box
15	说明	shuōmíng	动、名	to explain; directions
16	粒	lì	量	pills
17	服用	fúyòng	动	(of medicine) to take, to use
18	温	wēn	形	warm
19	开（水）	kāi（shuǐ）	动	to boil (water)
20	送	sòng	动	to send (here, to rinse down)
21	医院	yīyuàn	名	hospital
22	病	bìng	动、名	to feel ill; illness
23	医生	yīshēng	名	doctor
24	发烧	fā//shāo	(动宾)动	to have a fever
25	咳嗽	késou	动	to cough
26	后来	hòulái	名	afterwards, later
27	痰	tán	名	phlegm, sputum
28	张	zhāng	动	to open
29	嘴巴	zuǐba	名	mouth
30	发炎	fā//yán	(动宾)动	to show inflammation
31	验	yàn	动	to test
32	血	xiě	名	blood

33	化验	huàyàn	动	to test chemically
34	结果	jiéguǒ	名	result
35	病毒	bìngdú	名	virus
36	感染	gǎnrǎn	动、名	to infect, to be infected; infection
37	过敏	guòmǐn	动	to be allergic
38	打针	dǎ//zhēn	(动宾)动	to inject, to get an injection
39	输	shū	动	to infuse
40	液	yè	名	liquid
41	输液	shūyè		IV, intravenous drip
42	消炎	xiāo//yán	(动宾)动	to reduce inflammation
43	取	qǔ	动	to get, to take
44	休息	xiūxi	动	to rest, to sleep

四、词语解释 • Word Usage

开始不咳嗽，**后来**有一点儿，**现在**很厉害

汉语中，常用"开始……，后来……，现在……。"表示事情发展变化的过程。"开始……，后来……"两个小句中的内容都是指在过去发生过的事情或产生的状态。也可以只用"开始……，后来……"，常用来表示变化。

The pattern "开始…后来…现在…" is often used to indicate individual stages of a situation. The clauses following 开始 and 后来 describe situations or conditions in the past and are often used to indicate changes. "开始…后来…" can also be used alone.

例如：1. 来中国以后，开始我很不习惯，后来慢慢习惯了，现在我非常喜欢中国。
2. 开始是我不想去，后来是他不想去了。

我们来造句 • Make your own sentence

五、汉语知识 • Chinese Knowledge

肯定+否定的疑问形式 • The patterns "verb+不/没+verb" and "adjective+不/没+adjective"

汉语中，常用形容词或动词的肯定形式加否定形式（"不"或"没"）表达疑问的语气，相当于疑问词"吗"。这种形式在使用的时候只能是肯定在前，否定在后。比如"苹果大不大？（√）"是对的，"苹果不大大？（×）"是错的。双音节动词在使用时，可以只重复双音节中的前一个音节。比如"发不发烧"、"唱不唱歌"等。

Combining the positive and negative forms of a verb or an adjective is a common way to ask yes-or-no questions. The pattern is "verb+不/没+verb" or "adjective+不/没+adjective." For two syllable verbs, only the first character needs to be placed before 不 or 没, as in 发不发烧 and 唱不唱歌.

例如： 1. 我们一起去好不好？（意思是：我们一起去好吗？）
2. 你是不是留学生？（意思是：你是留学生吗？）
3. 你们有没有问题？（意思是：你们有问题吗?)
4. 你昨天打没打太极拳？（意思是：昨天你打太极拳了吗?)
5. 我们今天照不照相？（意思是：我们今天照相吗?)
6. 你愿不愿意教我汉语？（意思是：你愿意教我汉语吗?)

六、相关链接，有关生病的词语 • Related Terms: illness

1	肚子疼	dùziténg	to have a stomachache
2	呕吐	ǒutù	to vomit
3	拉肚子	lādùzi	to have diarrhea
4	头晕	tóuyūn	dizziness
5	喉咙疼	hóulóngténg	to have a sore throat
6	失眠	shī//mián	to lose sleep, to suffer from insomnia
7	脚扭了	jiǎoniǔle	to sprain or twist an ankle
8	牙疼	yáténg	to have a toothache; toothache
9	生病	shēng//bìng	to feel sick, to get sick

七、文化生活小贴士 • Tips for Daily Life: emergency numbers

1. 通用急救电话：120/110

   To call an ambulance, dial either 120 or 110.
2. 深圳大学校医院的电话：26537182 (day), 26537163 (night)

   To contact the campus infirmary, dial 26537182 during the day or 26537163 at night.

八、练习 • Exercises

（一）、填上合适的词语 • Fill in the blanks with appropriate words

取____、 ____、 ____疼

开____、 ____、 ____药

输____、 ____、 ____水

犯____、 ____、 ____结果

（二）、选词填空 • Fill in the blanks with the words provided

感冒　结果　考试　效果　说明　休息　过敏　化验

1. 今天有_____，所以大家都在准备。
2. _____还没出来，你先不要担心。
3. 听说这种药的_____不错，你试一试。
4. 下课_____的时候同学们在谈论考试的事。
5. 他_____了，挺严重的，在家休息呢。
6. 他不能吃海鲜，吃了以后会_____。
7. 药盒上有成份_____。
8. 今天验血，明天才能知道_____结果。

（三）、用所给词语完成句子 • Fill in the blanks with sentences using the words given in parentheses

1. A:这种药的成分是什么？
   B:_____。（说明）
2. A:你觉得汉语难吗？
   B:_____。（开始）
3. A:你习惯吃中国菜了吗？
   B:_____。（开始）
4. A:他今天怎么没来上课？
   B:_____。（疼）
5. A:医生给你开了什么药？
   B:_____。（盒）

（四）、解释下面句中"开"字的意思和用法

Explain the meaning of 开 in the following sentences

1. 请给我**开**张收据。
2. 学校附近的银行星期天不**开**门。
3. 请打**开**车门，我要下车。
4. 医生给他**开**了一些感冒药。
5. 泡茶要用**开**水。
6. 师傅，请您**开**快点儿，我有急事儿。

（五）、词语连线 • Match words to form short phrases

消　　取　　发　　张　　输　　验　　打

嘴　　药　　液　　炎　　烧　　针　　血

（六）、请你说一说下列病症的症状

Write the symptoms for each medical condition below

1. 肠胃炎 (gastroenteritis, stomach infection) _____
2. 感冒 (cold) _____
3. 皮肤过敏 (skin allergy) _____
4. 摔伤 (injury caused by falling) _____

（七）、用肯定+否定的疑问形式改写下列句子

Rewrite the following sentences using the pattern "verb+不/没+verb" or "adjective+不/没+adjective"

1. 你去深圳大学吗？ _____
2. 你是深圳大学的学生吗？ _____
3. 你学过汉语吗？ _____
4. 你喜欢打太极拳吗？ _____
5. 现在去来得及吗？ _____
6. 你明天上课吗？ _____
7. 你愿意教我汉语吗？ _____
8. 去深圳机场可以坐公交车吗？ _____

（八）、角色扮演 • Performance

利用相关链接里的词语，两人一组扮演医生和病人，互相问答。

Work in pairs. One student is a doctor. The other is a patient. Using the words in the "Related Terms" section, ask and answer questions about the patient's illness.

（九）、假如你现在感冒了，请写出一张请假条给老师并详细说明你的病情

Pretend that you have caught a cold. Write a letter to your teacher explaining your symptoms and asking for leave from class.

（十）、来聊天吧 • Discuss

1. 来中国以后你生过病吗？讲一段有关生病的故事。

   Since coming to China, have you fallen ill? Tell about any experiences you've had.

2. 你了解中国的医院吗？中国的医院和你们国家的一样吗？介绍一下你们国家医院的情况。

   Are you familiar with Chinese hospitals? Do Chinese hospitals differ from those in your home country? Tell us about your home country's hospitals.

3. 你知道中医的看病方法吗？在你们国家有中医医生吗？

   Do you know how Chinese doctors diagnose illnesses? Do doctors practice Chinese medicine in your home country?

第九课 / LESSON 9

我最喜欢大熊猫了
I LIKE THE GIANT PANDAS THE MOST

这一课我们将学到 • In this lesson we will study the following:
1. 与植物、动物有关的内容
2. 重点词语：怪不得、却、称……是……、
   一……就……
3. 辨析："但是（但）"和"却"
4. 汉语知识：汉语中的多音字

一、课文 • TEXT

（吴帅和艾美丽在仙湖植物园 • WuShuai and Emily are in the Fairy Lake botanical gardens）

 艾美丽： 欸，这些是什么花？红红的，真漂亮！
Hey, what sort of flowers are these? They're so red, and really beautiful.

 吴帅： 它叫簕杜鹃，是深圳市的市花。
They're called bougainvillea. They are Shenzhen's city flower.

 艾美丽： 那朵很香的花呢？
And that really fragrant one?

  吴帅： 那是白兰花。你知道吗，有很多花都可以泡茶喝，像蒲公英、茉莉、菊花、玫瑰等，这些茶闻起来很香，也非常好喝。
That is an orchid. You know, there are many flowers that all can be used to brew tea, like dandelions, jasmine, chrysanthemum, and roses. These teas smell very fragrant. They're also very good to drink.

 艾美丽： 我听说喝这些花泡的茶对身体很好。
I hear drinking tea brewed from these flowers is very good for your health.

 吴帅： 看到那棵很大的榕树了吗？就在你右边。
See that one really big banyan tree? It's just on your right.

 艾美丽： 看到了，怎么了？
I see it. What about it?

吴帅： 它是这里最老的一棵树，大概有200年了吧。
That is the oldest tree here, about 200 years old.

艾美丽： 嗯，怪不得他长了那么多"胡子"。
Umm, little wonder he's grown that many whiskers.

吴帅： 哈哈，你真会开玩笑。
Ha-ha, you really can make jokes.

吴帅和艾美丽在深圳野生动物园 • Wu Shuai and Emily are at the Shenzhen Safari park

吴帅： 你最想看什么动物？
Which animal do you most want to see?

艾美丽： 我最想看大熊猫、老虎和孔雀。
I most want to see the great pandas, the tigers, and the peacocks.

吴帅： 你喜欢大熊猫吗？
You like great pandas?

艾美丽： 嗯，我最喜欢大熊猫了。牠胖胖的，圆圆的，眼睛黑黑的，耳朵也黑黑的，肚子却白白的，看起来很可爱。
Umm, I like great pandas the most. They're so chubby and round. Their eyes are so black. Their ears are so black. But their stomachs are so white. They look very cute.

吴帅： 对，中国人称大熊猫是中国的国宝，有很多人都喜欢。
Right. Chinese people call great pandas China's national treasure. There are many people who like them.

艾美丽： 我从来没见过真的熊猫。对了，熊猫是熊还是猫？
I have never seen a real panda. Oh yeah, are pandas bears or cats?

吴帅： 牠是熊，不是猫。
They are bears. They are not cats.

艾美丽： 其实我也觉得牠比较像熊。
Actually, I also think they more resemble bears.

吴帅： 你家里养宠物吗？
Do you raise pets at home?

艾美丽： 嗯 我养一只猫、一条狗。一提起牠们我就想家了。
Umm, I raise a cat and a dog. As soon as they're mentioned, I miss home.

吴帅： 好了，好了，我们还是快去看大熊猫吧。
OK, OK, we'd best quickly got to see the great pandas, OK?

二、根据课文回答问题 • ANSWER THE FOLLOWING QUESTIONS ACCORDING TO THE TEXT

1. 深圳市的市花是什么？
   _____
2. 什么树长"胡子"？
   _____
3. 艾美丽最想看什么动物？
   _____
4. 中国人称大熊猫是什么？
   _____
5. 艾美丽以前见过大熊猫吗？
   _____
6. 吴帅一提养宠物艾美丽怎么了？
   _____

三、生词 • VOCABULARY

1	熊猫	xióngmāo	名	great panda, panda bear
2	植物	zhíwù	名	plant
3	园	yuán	名	garden
4	植物园	zhíwùyuán	名	botanical garden
5	簕杜鹃	lèdùjuān	名	bougainvillea
6	市	shì	名	city
7	朵	duǒ	量	[measure word, for single flowers]
8	香	xiāng	形	fragrant, odorous
9	白兰花	báilánhuā	名	orchid
10	泡	pào	动	to soak, (of tea) to brew
11	蒲公英	púgōngyīng	名	dandelion
12	茉莉	mòlì	名	jasmine
13	菊花	júhuā	名	chrysanthemum
14	闻	wén	动	to smell
15	好喝	hǎohē	形	(of drinks) good-tasting
16	身体	shēntǐ	名	body
17	棵	kē	量	[measure word, often for plants]
18	榕树	róngshù	名	banyan tree
19	树	shù	名	tree
20	怪不得	guàibude		little wonder…, no wonder…
21	长	zhǎng	动	to grow, to let grow
22	胡子	húzi	名	whiskers, beard
23	开玩笑	kāiwánxiào		to joke, to make a joke
24	野生	yěshēng		wild
25	动物	dòngwù	名	animal
26	动物园	dòngwùyuán	名	zoo

27	老虎	lǎohǔ	名	tiger
28	孔雀	kǒngquè	名	peacock
29	胖	pàng	形	fat
30	圆	yuán	形	round
31	眼睛	yǎnjīng	名	eye
32	耳朵	ěrduo	名	ear
33	肚子	dùzi	名	stomach
34	却	què	副	but, however
35	可爱	kěài	形	loveable, cute
36	称	chēng	动	to call
37	称……是……	chēng……shì……		[see Word Usage]
38	国（家）	guó（jiā）	名	country, nation
39	宝	bǎo	名	treasure
40	从来	cónglái	副	always
41	熊	xióng	名	bear
42	猫	māo	名	cat
43	其实	qíshí	副	actually, in reality
44	养	yǎng	动	to raise
45	宠物	chǒngwù	名	pet
46	只	zhī	量	[measure word, often for small animals]
47	狗	gǒu	名	dog
48	牠们	tāmen	代	(of animals) they, them
49	想（念）	xiǎng（niàn）	动	to think about, to miss

专名词 • Proper Names

50	仙湖植物园	xiānhúzhíwùyuán		"Fairy Lake" or Xianhu botanical garden
51	野生动物园	yěshēngdòngwùyuán		safari park

四、词语解释 • Word Usage

（一）、<u>怪不得</u>他长了那么多胡子

在这里，"怪不得"的意思是表示明白了出现某种情况或现象的原因。后面一句常会加上"原来……"，可独立成句。也可以说"难怪……"。

怪不得 indicates a sudden realization regarding a situation or a phenomenon. The clauses it introduces are often followed by another clause beginning with 原来. 难怪 has the same meaning and usage.

例如： 1. 怪不得他汉语说得那么好，原来他女朋友是中国人。
2. 难怪他看上去像生病一样，原来他已经三天没好好睡觉了。
3. A：他回国了，所以你没见到他。
   B：哦，怪不得。

我们来造句 • Make your own sentence

（二）、眼睛黑黑的，耳朵也黑黑的，肚子**却**白白的，看起来很可爱

汉语中，"却"表示转折。当连接两个小句子时，通常出现在第二个小句中，可出现在句首，也可出现在句子中间，但不能出现在主语前。

却 indicates a contrast. When joining two clauses, it appears in the second clause. It can appear either at the beginning or in the middle of a clause.

例如：1. 他比我出来得早，却比我到得晚。
2. 我喜欢红色，她却喜欢白色。
3. 他学了三年汉语，但却只学会了几十个汉字。

我们来造句 • Make your own sentence

（三）、中国人**称**大熊猫**是**中国的国宝

汉语中，常用"称……是……"表示称呼、命名人或事物、现象等。也可以用"称……为……"来表示，口语中也用"把……叫做……"。

The pattern "称…是…" indicates a person, thing, or phenomenon is referred to by a second title or nickname. The original name is placed after 称, and the nickname is placed after 是. "称…为…" and "把…叫做… have the same meaning.

例如：1. 人们也称出租车是"的士"。
2. 孩子们都称王老师是"妈妈"。
3. 人们称词典为工具书。

我们来造句 • Make your own sentence

（四）、**一** 提起它们（来）我**就**想家了

在这里，"一……就……"连接两个不同的动词，表示两种情况或现象发生的时间相隔很短，也表示一种情况或现象出现后一定会出现另一种情况或现象。

Here, the pattern "一…就…" links two verbs. It indicates that the second event takes place shortly after the first. It can also indicate that as soon as one situation occurs, a second quickly follows.

例如：1. 我一来他就走了。
2. 他一有问题就去问老师。

我们来造句 • Make your own sentence

○ 辨析：Distinguish between the following words

☞ "但是（但）"和"却"

汉语中，"但是（但）"、和"却"都表示转折，在连接两个小句子时，都出现在后面的小句子中，但"却"可以出现在句首，也可出现在句子

中间，而"但是（但）"只能出现在句首。"却"不能出现在主语前，"但是（但）"可以出现在主语前（例5，例6）。"却"可以和"但是（但）"同时使用（例6）。

但是（但）, and 却 all indicate a contrast. When used to join two clauses, all appear in the second clause. 却, however, can appear either at the beginning of or in the middle of a clause. 但是（但） can only appear at the beginning of a clause. When the second clause includes a subject, 却 must appear after, not before, the subject (5, 6). 却 can be used with both 但是（但）(6).

例如： 1. 他已经七十岁了，但走起路来像年轻人一样。
2. 他已经七十岁了，走起路来却像年轻人一样。
3. 他已经七十岁了，却像年轻人一样。
4. 我可以去，但你不能去。
5. 我可以去，你却不能去。
6. 这件事大家都知道，但他却不知道。

五、汉语知识 • Chinese Knowledge

汉语中的多音字

汉语中，很多字有两个或两个以上的读音。比如，"只有"的"只"和"一只猫"的"只"，写法完全一样，但读音却不一样。我们把这样的字称作"多音字"。

Many Chinese characters have more than one pronunciation. For example, the 只 in 只有 is pronounced in the 3rd tone. The 只 in 一只猫 is pronounced in the 1st tone. They are written the same, but pronounced differently. Such characters are called 多音字.

六、相关链接 • Related Terms: animals and plants

动物名称 • Names of animals

1	牛	niú	cow
2	马	mǎ	horse
3	羊	yáng	sheep
4	母鸡	mǔjī	hen
5	公鸡	gōngjī	rooster
6	猪	zhū	pig
7	鸭子	yāzi	duck
8	鸟	niǎo	bird
9	猴子	hóuzi	monkey
10	兔子	tùzi	rabbit
11	蛇	shé	snake
12	狮子	shīzi	lion
13	大象	dàxiàng	elephant
14	鱼	yú	fish
15	虾	xiā	shrimp

植物名称 • Names of plants

1	草	cǎo	grass
2	松树	sōngshù	pine
3	柳树	liǔshù	willow
4	竹子	zhúzi	bamboo
5	牡丹	mǔdān	peony
6	梅花	méihuā	plum blossom
7	康乃馨	kāngnǎixīn	carnation

七、文化生活小贴士 • CULTURAL TIPS: SHENZHEN PARKS

（一）、仙湖植物园

深圳仙湖植物园位于深圳市罗湖区东部，东边靠近梧桐山，西边靠近深圳水库，占地588公顷，始建于1983年，1988年5月1日正式对外开放，是一座集植物科学研究、物种迁徙地保存与展示、植物文化休闲以及生产应用等功能于一体的多功能风景园林植物园。仙湖植物园现建有17个植物专类区并收集有接近8000余种植物，植物种类保存量居全国同行前列。

The Fairy Lake Botanical Garden is located in the eastern part of Luohu. Its eastern edge is bordered by Wutong Mountain. Its western edge is bordered by Shenzhen's reservoir. It occupies 588 hectares. It was started in 1983 and opened to the public on May 1st, 1988. It is a center for botanical and conservation research. It is also a beautiful sight-seeing destination. The botanical gardens include 17 different sections with nearly 8,000 plant species. It is at the leading edge of botanical gardens in the country.

Bus: 公交 – 113路空调 – 出发：深圳大学 – 下车站：罗湖外语学校；

Taxi: 90元左右

（二）、深圳动物园

深圳野生动物园是中国第一家放养式的野生动物园，建于山清水秀的深圳西丽湖畔，占地面积60多万平方米，这是一个引人入胜的神奇地方，园内有奇异多姿的飞禽走兽，幽雅恬静的自然环境，布局独特的园林设计。

The Shenzhen Safari Park is the first safari park built in China. It was built near beautiful Xili Lake, it occupies more than 600, 000 square meters. The layout of the park is unique. Here, visitors can watch many exotic animals in a peaceful, natural environment.

Bus: 公交 74路空调 – 出发：深圳大学 – 下车站：直升机场 – 转公交 226路 – 出发：直升机场（朗山路） – 下车站：动物园；Taxi：50元左右

八、练习 • EXERCISES

（一）、填上合适的词语 • Fill in the blanks with appropriate words

泡_____、_____　　养_____、_____

长_____、_____　　想_____、_____

（二）、选词填空 • Fill in the blanks with the words provided

▶ 从来　　却　　其实　　比较　　怪不得　　称……是

1. 他看上去身体很好，_____经常生病。

2. 他生病_____不去医院，总是吃点儿药就算了。

3. _____他那么胖，因为他从来不运动。

4. 本来应该_____"熊猫"_____"猫熊"。

5. 我最近_____忙，不能跟你去动物园玩儿了。

6. 去植物园的主意是他出的，可现在他_____不去了。

▶ 但是　却

1. 他只有两岁，_____认识一百多个汉字。

2. 我喜欢红色，她_____喜欢白色。

3. 我想明天去游泳，_____他想今天去。

4. 我来找他，他_____走了。

（三）、用所给词语完成句子 • Fill in the blanks with sentences using the words given in parentheses

1. A：你喜欢兔子吗？
   B：_____。（……起来）

2. A：听说他生病了。
   B：_____。（怪不得）

3. A：大部分中国人都喜欢红色。
   B：_____。（却）

4. A：你染过头发吗？
   B：_____。（从来）

5. A：你的朋友真有意思。
   B：_____。（开玩笑）

6. A：你跟他真的很熟悉吗？
   B：_____。（其实）

（四）、词语连线 • Match words to form short phrases

耳朵　　　眼睛　　　嘴巴　　　鼻子

看　　　　说　　　　听　　　　闻

（五）、列出中国十二生肖，并试着用"圆圆的、黑黑的、白白的、红红的"等词语描述他们的特征

List the twelve animals of the Chinese Zodiac. Use adjectives like 圆圆的, 黑黑的, 白白的, and 红红的 to describe them.

（六）、说说你最喜欢和最讨厌的动物、植物是什么？为什么？

Which are your favorite animals and plants? Which are your least favorite animals and plants? Why?

（七）、看植物图片，认读植物名称

Look at the pictures below. Read the name of each plant aloud

（八）、来聊天吧 • Discuss

1. 说一个跟养动物有关的故事。

   Tell a story about raising pets.

2. 你们国家的国花是什么？介绍一下它的特点。

   What is your national flower? Tell about its special characteristics.

（九）、猜一猜：它们是什么？ • Guess what it is

提示：以下所有动物植物都在本课出现过。
Tip: All of the animals and plants appear in this book

▶ 猜动物 • Guess the animal
1. 脸上长鼻子，头上挂扇子，四根粗柱子，一条小辫子。
2. 头戴大红花，身穿什锦衣，好像当家人，一早催人起。
3. 粽子头，梅花脚，屁股挂把指挥刀，坐着反比立着高。
4. 年纪并不大，胡子一大把，不论遇见谁，总爱喊妈妈。
5. 一把刀，水里漂，有眼睛，没眉毛。
6. 嘴像小铲子，脚像小扇子，走路左右摆，不是摆架子。
7. 八字须，往上翘，说话好像娃娃叫，只洗脸，不梳头，夜行不用灯光照。
8. 身体花绿，走路弯曲，洞里进出，开口恶毒。
9. 上肢下肢都是手，有时爬来有时走，走时很像一个人，爬时又像一条狗。
10. 像熊比熊小，像猫比猫大，竹笋是食粮，密林中安家。
11. 小小船，白布篷。头也红，桨也红。
12. 耳朵长，尾巴短，红眼睛，白毛衫，三瓣嘴儿胆子小，青菜萝卜吃个饱。
13. 性情躁烈爆，常披黄皮袄，山中称大王，我说那是猫。
14. 任劳又任怨，田里活猛干，生产万吨粮，只把草当饭。
15. 说它像鸡不是鸡，尾巴长长拖到地，张开尾巴像把扇，花花绿绿真美丽。

▶ 趣味谜语 • Interesting riddles
1. 一片大草地 （猜一植物）
   来了一群羊 （猜一水果）
   来了一群狼 （猜一水果）
   又来了一群老虎 （打一种水果）
   老虎走后来了一头羊和一只狼，狼没有吃羊 （打一海产动物）
   这时又过来一只狼，还是没有吃羊 （再打一海产动物）
   一会儿又过来一只狼，羊对狼叫了一声．狼还是没有吃羊 （还是一海产动物）
2. 头上青丝如针刺，皮肤厚裂像龟甲，越是寒冷越昂扬，一年四季精神好。
3. 小时青青腹中空，长大头发蓬蓬松，姐姐撑船不离它，哥哥钓鱼拿手中。
4. 天南地北都能住，春风给我把辫梳，溪畔湖旁搭凉棚，能撒雪花当空舞。
5. 花中君子艳而香，空谷佳人美名扬，风姿脱俗堪钦佩，纵使无人也自芳。
6. 得天独厚艳而香，国色天香美名扬，不爱攀附献媚色，何惧飘落到他乡。
7. 小小伞兵随风飞，飞到东来飞到西，降落路边田野里，安家落户扎根基。
8. 有叶不开花，开花不见叶，花开百花前，飘香傲风雪。

第十课
LESSON 10

我们一起出去庆祝一下吧！
WE'LL GO OUT TOGETHER AND CELEBRATE, OK?

这一课我们将学到 • In this lesson we will study the following:
1. 庆祝生日以及与深圳KTV有关的内容
2. 重点词语：不但……而且……、如果……就……、可以男、女生对唱、光、虽然……但是……、……来着
3. 汉语知识：（1）趋向动词"来"和"去"
　　　　　　（2）汉语中的复句

一、课文 • Text

（课间休息时 • During a break between classes）

 艾美丽的同学： 今天是你的生日，晚上我们一起出去庆祝一下吧！
Today is your birthday. Tonight, we'll go out together and celebrate, OK?

 艾美丽： 好啊，但是我对深圳的娱乐场所不熟悉，你有什么好建议呢？
OK, but I'm not that familiar with Shenzhen's entertainment venues. What good suggestions do you have?

 艾美丽的同学： 我经常和我的朋友去海岸城的KTV。我们去那儿唱歌吧。
I always go with my friends to Coastal City's KTV [karaoke center]. We'll go together and sing, OK?

 艾美丽： 好啊！
OK.

 艾美丽： 太好了！我还没去过中国的KTV。那里环境怎么样？
Great. I still haven't gone to a Chinese KTV. How is the ambiance there?

 艾美丽的同学： 不但环境不错，而且价格合理。如果有会员卡就更便宜了。
Not only is the ambiance not bad, but also the prices are reasonable. If you have a membership card, then it's even more inexpensive.

艾美丽： 嗯，就这么定了！我约我的男朋友一起去，他也一定很想参加。
Umm, then it's decided. I'll invite my boyfriend to go with us. He'll also certainly want to join us.

吴帅、艾美丽和朋友们来到一家KTV • Wu Shuai, Emily, and friends arrive at the KTV

服务员： 欢迎光临，请问几位？
Welcome here. May I ask how many people?

吴帅： 我们八位。
We're eight people.

服务员： 好的。那就来间大房吧。
OK. Then you'll want to rent a large room, right?

吴帅： 今天是这位小姐的生日，请问有什么优惠的？
Today is this young lady's birthday. May I ask what special treatment you have?

服务员： 哦。有的。我们可以免费赠送一盘水果，一支香槟。同时，还可以免费帮您办理一张会员卡，平时可以享受八折优惠。你们想唱几个小时？
Oh, we do have some. We can give you one plate of fruit and a bottle of sparkling wine free of charge. We can also help you register for a membership card free of charge. With it, most of the time you can enjoy a 20% discount. You want to sing for how many hours?

吴帅： 那我们唱三个小时吧。
We'll sing for three hours, OK?

服务员： 好的。打折后一共是120块钱。我们的工作人员会带你们去房间。
OK, after the discount, altogether it is 120 RMB. Our staff will take you to your room.

在KTV房间 • In a KTV room

吴帅： 这里不但有很多经典歌曲，而且还有很多流行歌曲，你可以看看排行榜。
Here, they not only have many classic songs, but they also have many popular songs. You can look at the top song listings.

艾美丽： 哦！还有不少英文歌，怪不得很多留学生来中国以后喜欢来KTV唱歌。
Oh, they also have more than a few English songs. No wonder so many overseas students like to come to KTV to sing after they've come to China!

吴帅： 我来帮你点歌。你唱一首什么歌？
I'll help you order a song. What song are you singing?

艾美丽：我刚在口语课上学了一首《月亮代表我的心》，我想复习一下儿。
In Kouyu class, I just studied one song, "The Moon Represents My Heart." I want to go over it.

吴帅：好啊，这首歌可以男、女生对唱，我们俩一起唱好不好？
OK, this song can be sung together by a man and a woman. The two of us can sing together, OK?

艾美丽：好，没问题。
Good. No problem.

艾美丽的同学：你可别光唱歌，今天可是你的生日，大家举杯庆祝一下儿吧。
You absolutely can't only sing. Today is your birthday. Everybody raise your glass and celebrate, right?

艾美丽的同学：对，艾美丽你要多喝点儿。
That's right. Emily, you have to drink.

艾美丽：虽然我不会喝酒，但是今天一定要喝。我听说中国人开心喝酒的时候喜欢那个什么来着？——
Although I can't really drink much, today I certainly should drink. I hear that Chinese people, when they're having a good time drinking, like to (say) … What was it?--

艾美丽的同学："不醉不归"！"不醉不归"！对，对……
"If you aren't drunk, don't go home." "If you aren't drunk, don't go home." Right, right…

吴帅：服务员，来一打青岛啤酒！
Waitress, bring a dozen Tsingtao beers!

艾美丽的同学：来，大家举杯。祝我们亲爱的艾美丽小姐生日快乐！同时，也为我们的友谊干杯！
Come on, everybody raise your glass. Wish our dear Miss Emily, "Happy Birthday." At the same time, drink to our friendship. Bottoms up!

大家举杯 • Everyone raises a glass

同学们：干杯！
Bottoms up!

二、根据课文回答问题 • ANSWER THE FOLLOWING QUESTIONS ACCORDING TO THE TEXT

1. 艾美丽过生日，同学们建议艾美丽怎么庆祝？

   _____

2. 艾美丽过生日，KTV给艾美丽什么优惠了？

   _____

3. 留学生来中国以后为什么都喜欢去KTV唱歌？
   _____

4. 同学们建议艾美丽喝点儿酒，艾美丽怎么说？
   _____

5. 艾美丽在口语课上学了一首什么歌？
   _____

6. "不醉不归"是什么意思？
   _____

三、生词 • Vocabulary

1	庆祝	qìngzhù	动	to celebrate
2	课间	kèjiān		break between classes
3	生日	shēngri	名	birthday
4	娱乐	yúlè	动、名	to entertain; entertainment, recreation
5	场所	chángsuǒ	名	place, venue
6	唱歌	chàng//gē	(动宾)动	to sing
7	环境	huánjìng	名	environment, atmosphere, ambiance
8	不但……而且……	búdàn……érqiě……		not only… but also …
9	价格	jiàgé	名	price, cost
10	合理	hélǐ	形	reasonable
11	如果……就……	rúguǒ……jiù……		if…then…
12	会员	huìyuán	名	member, membership
13	男	nán	名	male
14	一定	yídìng	副	certainly
15	参加	cānjiā	动	to join, to take part in
16	赠送	zèngsòng	动	(of a gift) to give
17	盘	pán	量	[a measure word, dish, plate]
18	支	zhī	量	[a measure word for long, thin objects]

19	香槟	xiāngbīn	名	sparkling wine, Champagne (wine)
20	同时	tóngshí	副	at the same time
21	平时	píngshí	名	most of the time
22	享受	xiǎngshòu	动	to enjoy, to be satisfied
23	唱	chàng	动	to sing
24	小时	xiǎoshí	量	[a measure word, hour]
25	经典	jīngdiǎn	名、形	classics; classic, classical
26	歌曲	gēqǔ	名	song
27	流行	liúxíng	动、形	to deem popular; popular
28	排行	páiháng	名	(of brothers and sisters) seniority
29	榜	bǎng	名	list of names
30	排行榜	páihángbǎng		here, song listings
31	英文	yīngwén	名	the English language
32	歌	gē	名	song
33	首	shǒu	量	[a measure word for songs and poems]
34	口语	kǒuyǔ	名	spoken language, speaking
35	月亮	yuèliang	名	the moon
36	代表	dàibiǎo	动、名	to represent; representation
37	心	xīn	名	heart
38	复习	fùxí	动	to review, to go over again
39	女	nǚ	名	female
40	女生	nǚshēng	名	female student
41	俩	liǎ		two
42	光	guāng	副	only, just
43	举	jǔ	动	to raise, to lift
44	杯	bēi	名	glass, cup
45	虽然……但是……	suīrán……dànshì……		although…still…
46	酒	jiǔ	名	alcohol
47	……来着	……láizhe		[see Word Usage]
48	醉	zuì	动	drunk, intoxicated
49	归	guī	动	to return (home)

50	不醉不归	búzuìbùguī		[literally, "Not drunk, no return (home)"]
51	打	dá	量	[a measure word, a dozen]
52	祝	zhù	动	to wish, to bless
53	亲爱的	qīn'àide		dear, beloved
54	快乐	kuàilè	形	happy, joyful
55	为	wèi	介	for, on behalf of
56	友谊	yǒuyì	名	friendship
57	干	gān	形	dry
58	干杯	gānbēi		[literally, "Dry glass.": a toast meaning people should to finish drinking an entire glass]

专名词 • Proper Names

| 59 | 海岸城 | hǎi'ànchéng | Coastal City |
| 60 | 青岛 | qīngdǎo | Qingdao (a city); Tsingtao beer [Note: "Tsingtao" is also pronounced "qīngdǎo." "Tsingtao" is a transliteration using the now rarely used EFEO system.] |

四、词语解释 • Word Usage

（一）、不但……而且……

"不但……而且……"常常用来连接两个小句子，表示除所说的以外还有别的情况。当两个小句是同一个主语时，"不但"放在第一个小句的主语后，当两个小句是不同的主语时，"不但"放在第一个小句的主语前。另外，"不但……而且……"也可以连接两个名词性的词语或介词短语。

The pattern "不但…而且…"is often used to link two clauses. It indicates that, in addition to one situation or quality, another situation or quality exists. When the subject in both clauses is the same, 不但 is placed after the subject in the first clause, and 而且 is placed at the beginning of the second clause (1). When the 2 clauses have different subjects, both 不但 and 而且 are placed before the subjects (2). "不但…而且…" can also link two noun phrases (3) or two prepositional phrases (4).

例如： 1. 他不但会打网球，而且会踢足球。
2. 不但我喜欢他，而且大家都喜欢他。
3. 不但孩子，而且大人也喜欢唱这首歌。
4. 不但在我们班，而且在所有的班讲这件事。

我们来造句 • Make your own sentence

___

（二）、如果……就……

"如果……就……"常常用来连接两个小句子，前一个小句是假设出现的情况，后一个小句是根据假设推断出的结论或提出的问题。

The pattern "如果…就…" is often used to link two clauses. The first clause states a condition. The second clause states an outcome of the previously stated condition's being met.

　　例如：1. 如果今天下雨，我们就不去买东西了。
　　　　　2. 如果他不来，怎么办？

我们来造句 • Make your own sentence

___

（三）、这首歌也可以男、女生对唱

在这里，"对"表示相反、相比、相关的关系。"……男、女生对唱"的意思是，一首歌由男、女两个人（或两种声音）合唱，有的部分可以一人一句，也可以一人一段，也有的部分可以合唱。这种用法也常常表示比赛的双方。

Here, 对 indicates opposition or alternation. "男，女生对唱" is a duet sung by a man and a woman, or sung with male and female voices. Singers may alternate singing lines or sections and, at times, may sing together. 对 can also be used when listing the opponents in a competition.

　　例如：1. 我刚学了一首对唱歌曲，我们俩一起唱吧。
　　　　　2. 今天的篮球比赛是留学生队对中国学生队。

我们来造句 • Make your own sentence

___

（四）、你可别光唱歌

在这里，"光"是副词，表示只做一件事、一个动作或一直做一件事、一个动作。相当于"只"的意思。常用于口语。

Here, 光 is an adverb. It indicates that only one action is being concentrated on at one time. It is comparable to 只 in this use and is often used in speech.

　　例如：1. 他光喝酒不吃饭。
　　　　　2. 别光看书，我们出去玩儿会儿吧。

我们来造句 • Make your own sentence

（五）、虽然……但是……

汉语中，"虽然"表示让步，"但是"表示转折。前一小句的意思是承认句子中说的是事实，后一小句的意思是情况不会因为前面的事实而不出现或发生改变。

In the pattern "虽然…但是…," 虽然 indicates a concession or admission, while 但是 indicates a contradiction or transition. The first clause states a fact. The second clause describes a situation that will not or does not change even as a result of the previously stated fact.

例如： 1. 虽然他没有很多钱，但是他很快乐。
2. 虽然汉语很难学好，但我还是要学。

我们来造句 • Make your own sentence

_____

（六）、那个什么来着？

"……来着"表示曾经发生过什么事。用于口语，出现在句末。因为是表示已经发生的事情，所以句中的动词不能带表示结果、完成意思的词语，也没有否定的形式。

来着 indicates that an action or situation has occurred before. In speech, it appears at the end of a sentence. Because it indicates only an occurrence or experience, it is not used with words indicating actions' completion or results. There is no negative form.

例如： 1. 我刚才去打球来着。
2. 你昨天说什么来着？

我们来造句 • Make your own sentence

_____

五、汉语知识 • Chinese Knowledge

（一）、趋向动词"来"和"去" The directional verbs 来 and 去

汉语中的趋向动词"来"和"去"，常出现在一些句中的主要动词后，表示主要动词的趋向。比如："出来"、"出去"、"上来"、"上去"等等。以说话人的位置为中心，"来"表示朝说话人的方向而来，"去"表示离说话人的方向而去。比如，一个人在房间里，他要离开房间的时候说"我出去。"而站在房间外面的人叫他时，就要说"你出来。"同样，一个人在楼上，他叫楼下的人，就说"你上来。"而楼下的人就会说"我上去。"正确理解和使用"来"和"去"，重要的是记住"以说话人的位置为中心"。

来 and 去 often appear after the main verb in a sentence. They indicate the "direction" in which a verb is performed. Such "directions" are interpreted based on the position of the speaker at the time of speaking. As one illustration, one person is leaving a room, while another person is calling for him to leave the room. The person leaving the room would say, "我出去," while the person calling him to leave the room would say, "你出来." As another example, a man is on the top of a building, while a woman is standing at the bottom. If the man calls for the woman to come to the top of the building, he would say, "你上来." If the woman agrees to go to the top of the building, she would say, "我上去."

（二）、汉语中的复句 • Correlative sentences

汉语中，把两个意义相关的小句子连接起来，组成的一个大句子，叫复句。表示两个小句子之间关系的词语叫关联词。例如："虽然……但是……"、"如果……就……"、"不但……而且……"等都是复句。"如果"、"就""不但"、"而且"、"虽然"、"但是"等都是关联词。

In Chinese, 复句 are sentences formed with more than one clause and joined with specific words called 关联词. [关联词 is usually translated in English simply as "conjunctions," though in this context the translation "correlative conjunctions" may help students better remember the usage.] The patterns "虽然…但是…","如果…就…," and "不但……而且……"are all 复句. 如果， 就， 不但， 而且， 虽然， and 但是 are all 关联词.

六 、相关链接 • RELATED TERMS AND INFORMATION

（一）、与过生日有关的词语 • Words related to birthdays

1	贺卡	hèkǎ	greeting card
2	蛋糕	dàngāo	cake
3	蜡烛	làzhú	candle
4	许愿	xǔ//yuàn	to make a wish, to make a vow
5	晚会	wǎnhuì	party

（二）、歌曲《月亮代表我的心》的歌词 • Lyrics to "The Moon Represents my Heart"

- 你问我爱你有多深，我爱你有几分。
- 我的情也真，我的爱也真，月亮代表我的心。
- 你问我爱你有多深，我爱你有几分，我的情不移（移, yí, to change），我的爱不变（变, biàn, to change），月亮代表我的心。
- 轻轻的一个吻（吻, wěn, a kiss），已经打动（to move）我的心，深深的一段情，叫我思念到如今，你问我爱你有多深，我爱你有几分，你去想一想，你去看一看，月亮代表我的心。

七、文化生活小贴士 • Tips for Daily Life: Shenzhen KTVs

（一）、关于深圳的KTV About KTVs in Shenzhen

深圳一般的KTV有几种房间：迷你房，小房，中房，大房，PARTY房，VIP房等；每家KTV的收费标准不同，有的按小时算，有的按人数算，有的按时段算等。深圳比较有名的KTV有：钱柜（qiánguì）、BBFLY KTV、加州红（jiāzhōuhóng）、天籁村（tiānlàicūn）、k-box。

Shenzhen's KTVs have different types of rooms, such as mini rooms, small rooms, medium rooms, large rooms, "party" rooms, and VIP rooms. Each KTV may have different ways of charging rates, such as per hour, per other measure of time, or per person. Some of Shenzhen's relatively well-known KTVs are 钱柜, BBFLY KTV, 加州红, 天籁村, and K-box.

（二）、深圳比较有名的酒吧 • Some relatively well-known Shenzhen bars

苏荷吧（sūhébā）　　　　SOHO.BAR　　　　（罗湖区）
乐巢（lècháo）　　　　　Le Nest Club　　　　（罗湖区）
本色（běnsè）　　　　　True Color Club　　　（罗湖区）
根据地（gēnjùdì）　　　　Base Bar　　　　　（南山区，罗湖区）

八、练习 • Exercises

（一）、填上合适的词语 • Fill in the blanks with appropriate words

举_____、_____　　　　流行_____、_____
喝_____、_____　　　　复习_____、_____
娱乐_____、_____　　　　价格_____、_____
不醉_____

（二）、选词填空 • Fill in the blanks with the words provided

▶ 庆祝　环境　享受　参加　流行　赠送　合理　场所

1. 我刚租了一套房子，虽然很贵，但_____很好。
2. 他很喜欢自己的工作，_____到很多工作的快乐。
3. 大家聚在一起为小王_____生日。
4. 这瓶酒不是我们点的，是饭馆_____的。
5. 现在是_____感冒发病的高峰期。
6. 这家饭馆的饭菜味道不错，价格也_____。
7. 他不喜欢唱歌，深圳的娱乐_____他从来没去过。
8. 为了_____同学的生日会她穿了一条很漂亮的裙子。

▶ 一定　　为了　　光　　……来着　　平时　　同时

1. _____我中午在学校的餐厅吃饭，周末在家吃饭。
2. 他从来没见过下雪，_____看雪，他下星期去哈尔滨。
3. 大家都在等你，你_____要来！
4. 今天上课老师说什么_____？
5. _____喝酒不吃饭对身体不好。
6. 为了赚钱，他_____做两份工作。

（三）、用所给词语完成句子

Fill in the blanks with sentences using the words given in parentheses

1. A：深圳夏天的天气怎么样？
   B：_____。（不但……而且……）
2. A：_____？（……来着）
   B：我也忘了，你去问小张吧。
3. A：你不喜欢我为什么还要帮我？
   B：_____。（虽然……但是……）
4. A：能不能便宜点儿？
   B：_____。（如果……就……）
5. A：你为什么住学校的留学生宿舍？
   B：_____。（为）

（四）、使用划线词语仿造例句造句

Use the underlined words to form sentences

1. 深圳大学<u>不但</u>环境好，<u>而且</u>同学、老师也都很好。
2. <u>如果</u>明天下雨，<u>就</u>不去游泳了。
3. <u>虽然</u>汉字很难，<u>但是</u>很有意思。
4. 他刚来深圳，所以<u>对</u>深圳大学附近的情况还<u>不熟悉</u>。

（五）、填量词 • Choose from the measure words provided to fill in the blanks

打　　首　　条　　粒　　盘　　朵　　只　　棵

一____围巾　　一____歌　　一____啤酒
一____花　　　一____药　　一____树
一____水果　　一____猫

（六）、指出下列句子中"对"的意义或用法

Explain the meaning of 对 in the following sentences

1. 你说得<u>对</u>。
2. <u>对</u>了，我们在机场见过面。
3. 人民币<u>对</u>美元的汇率是多少？
4. 我<u>对</u>这个问题不感兴趣。
5. 他<u>对</u>深圳很熟悉。
6. 这首歌是男女<u>对</u>唱的。

（七）、根据下面的图表选择一个KTV房间，说说为什么？

Based on the following chart, select a KTV room for an event and explain your choice

（八）、请一位同学唱一首汉语歌，大家说一说歌的内容

Anyone who can sing a Chinese song, please volunteer to sing for the class. The rest of the class should try to explain the song's meaning.

（九）、来聊天吧 • Discuss

1. 你喜欢怎么庆祝生日？为什么？

   How do you like to celebrate your birthday? Why?

2. 你一般送朋友什么生日礼物？

   What kinds of birthday present do you usually give to friends?

3. 介绍一家娱乐场所给同学们或介绍一下你们国家娱乐场所的情况。

   Tell the class about an entertainment venue or about what entertainment venues are common in your home country.

第十一课 / LESSON 11

深圳是个什么样的城市?
WHAT SORT OF CITY IS SHENZHEN?

这一课我们将学到 • In this lesson we will study the following:
1. 有关深圳这个城市的内容
2. 重点词语：来自、别看、既……又……、
   不仅……而且……
3. 汉语知识：（1）汉语的普通话
              （2）汉语中的成语

一、课文 • Text

（艾美丽和金美善是好朋友，她们在网上聊天 • Emily and Kim Mee-Seon are friends. They are chatting online）

美善： 嗨，艾美丽！
Hi, Emily!

艾美丽： 唉，美善！
Hey, Mei Shan!

美善： 你汉语说得越来越好，真羡慕你。
Your Chinese speaking is better and better. I really admire you.

艾美丽： 是啊，我自己也觉得进步挺大的。你也来深圳大学吧，那样我们又可以常常见面了。
It is. I, myself, also think that my progress has been big. You should also come to Shenzhen University. That way, we can often see each other.

美善： 我也非常怀念我们在一起的日子。深圳是个什么样的城市？外国人多吗？
I also really cherish the memory of the days we were together. What sort of city is Shenzhen? Are there many foreigners?

艾美丽： 当然，很多外国人在这里学汉语，也有很多外国人来这里投资。
Of course. Many foreigners are here studying Chinese. Also, there are many foreigners who come here to invest.

美善： 你觉得深圳的什么最吸引外国人？
What about Shenzhen do you think most attracts foreigners?

艾美丽： 每个人的感觉不一样吧。比如，深圳靠近香港，很多人觉得去香港很方便，回国也很方便。
Every person's feelings are not the same. For example, Shenzhen is close to Hong Kong, and many people think going to Hong Kong is very convenient. Returning to your home country is also convenient.

美善： 听说深圳是个移民城市，就像旧金山、新加坡一样。
I have heard that Shenzhen is an immigrant city, just like San Francisco and Singapore.

艾美丽： 没错。这里有来自中国各地的人，所以大家都说普通话。
That's right. Here we have many people from all parts of China, so everyone speaks Putonghua.

美善： 我听说深圳是个年轻的城市。
I have heard that Shenzhen is a young city.

艾美丽： 你别看它历史不长，但是很发达，既漂亮又繁华。
You shouldn't just look at the fact that its history is not long. It's very developed. Also, it's both beautiful and busy.

美善： 对了，你是购物狂，那里买东西方便吗？
Oh, yeah! You're a shopping maniac. Is buying things there convenient?

艾美丽： 在深圳买东西很方便，有很多购物广场。
In Shenzhen, buying things is very convenient. We have many shopping malls.

美善： 真好，我也喜欢逛街。可是，那里有韩国菜吗？我恐怕不习惯吃中国菜。
Really good. I also like shopping. But, do you have Korean food there? I'm afraid I'm not used to eating Chinese food.

艾美丽： 当然有。在深圳不仅有很多中餐馆，而且还有世界各国不同风味的餐厅。你想吃什么菜都有。
Of course we do. In Shenzhen, not only are there many Chinese restaurants, but there are also restaurants with flavors from every country in the world. Whatever food you want to eat we have.

美善： 太棒了！另外，那儿有什么好玩儿的地方吗？
Too great! Aside from that, do you have any fun places there?

艾美丽： 我想想……世界之窗、锦绣中华、欢乐谷，这些景点都不错啊，在那里，你可以参观全世界、全中国的风景名胜。
Let me think… Window on the World, Splendid China, and Happy Valley. These scenic spots are all not bad. There, you can visit all of the world's and all of China's tourist destinations.

美善： 听你这么说，我现在就想去深圳。
Hearing what you say, now I want to go to Shenzhen.

 艾美丽： 你决定了以后给我打电话，到深圳以后我去机场接你。
After you decide, give me a telephone call. After you arrive in Shenzhen, I'll go to the airport and pick you up.

 美善： 好的，一言为定。
OK. Consider it settled.

二、根据课文回答问题 • Answer the following questions according to the text

1. 美善羡慕艾美丽什么？
   _____

2. 深圳外国人多吗？他们来深圳做什么？
   _____

3. 深圳大部分人说什么话？
   _____

4. 艾美丽非常喜欢做什么？
   _____

5. 美善担心来深圳哪方面不习惯？
   _____

6. 深圳有什么好玩的地方？
   _____

7. 听艾美丽介绍以后美善觉得深圳怎么样？
   _____

8. 艾美丽觉得深圳是个什么样的城市？
   _____

三、生词 • Vocabulary

1	什么样	shénmeyàng		what sort, what type, what kind
2	城市	chéngshì	名	city
3	网	wǎng	名	the Internet
4	聊天儿	liáo//tiānr	(动宾)动	to chat
5	嗨	hāi	叹	[an exclamation: "Hi"]
6	唉	āi	叹	[an exclamation: "Hey"]
7	羡慕	xiànmù	动	to admire
8	进步	jìnbù	动、名	to improve; progress

9	怀念	huáiniàn	动、名	to cherish a memory
10	日子	rìzi	名	day
11	投资	tóuzī	动、名	to invest; investment
12	吸引	xīyǐn	动、名	to attract; attraction
13	移民	yímín	名、动	to migrate, to immigrate; immigrant
14	自	zì	介	from
15	来自	láizì		to come from
16	全	quán	形	all, complete
17	各地	gèdì		every place
18	话	huà	名	speech
19	普通话	pǔtōnghuà		Mandarin Chinese
20	年轻	niánqīng	形	young
21	历史	lìshǐ	名	history
22	发达	fādá	形	economically developed
23	既……又……	jì……yòu……		not only…but also…
24	繁华	fánhuá	形	busy, bustling
25	物	wù	名	thing, matter, substance
26	购物	gòuwù		shopping
27	……狂	……kuáng	名	maniac, fanatic
28	广场	guǎngchǎng	名	mall, plaza
29	逛	guàng	动	to stroll, to wander
30	街	jiē	名	street
31	逛街	guàngjiē		to shop
32	恐怕	kǒngpà	副	be afraid, fear, perhaps
33	不仅……而且……	bùjǐn……érqiě……		not only… but also…
34	中餐	zhōngcān	名	Chinese restaurant
35	世界	shìjiè	名	world
36	各国	gèguó		every country
37	风味	fēngwèi	名	flavor
38	棒	bàng	形	great, awesome, excellent
39	好玩儿	hǎowǎnr	形	fun
40	景点	jǐngdiǎn	名	tourist spot
41	风景	fēngjǐng	名	scenery
42	名胜	míngshèng	名	scenic spot
43	决定	juédìng	动、名	to decide; decision
44	接	jiē	动	to pick up, to meet

专名词 • Proper Names

45	金美善	jīnměishàn	Kim Mee-Seon
46	香港	xiānggǎng	Hong Kong
47	新加坡	xīnjiāpō	Singapore
48	旧金山	jiùjīnshān	San Francisco
49	世界之窗	shìjièzhīchuāng	Window on the World
50	锦绣中华	jǐnxiùzhōnghuá	Splendid China
51	欢乐谷	huānlègǔ	Happy Valley

四、词语解释 • Word Usage

（一）、那里有<u>来自</u>中国各地的人

"来自"的意思是"从……来"，表示一个人的故乡或国籍，也可表示事物的出处或消息的来源。后面通常接表示地方、处所的词，也可以接表示人的词。表示事物的出处或消息的来源时，也可用"产自"、"出自"等。

来自 has the same meaning as "从…来." It indicates a person is from another city or country. It can also indicate where items or news originated. It is usually followed by the name of a place or person. When discussing the origins of items or news, words like 产自 and 出自 can also be used.

例如：
1. 他来自广州，我来自北京。
2. 这个消息来自小王。
3. 这种水果产自北方。
4. 这句话出自一本书。

我们来造句 • Make your own sentence

_____

（二）、你<u>别看</u>它历史不长，……

在这里，"别看"的意思是"不要只看、不要认为"。它常常出现在前面的小句子里，意思是"不要看表面的现象、不要只根据已经知道的某些情况做出判断"，而后面小句子的意思是说明真实的情况是什么样的。

Here, 别看 has the same meaning as 不要只看 or 不要认为. It often appears in the first of two clauses and suggests we look not only at the surface of things or rely only upon what we know of a subject when forming opinions. The second clause describes the true nature of the subject under discussion.

例如：
1. 别看他只有3岁，但他能写80多个汉字。
2. 别看他嘴上不说，但心里都明白。

我们来造句 • Make your own sentence

_____

（三）、既……又……

"既……又……"表示同时具有两个方面的性质或情况。常连接两个动词或两个形容词。

The pattern "既…又…" indicates that two aspects or qualities exist at the same time. It is often used to link two verbs or two adjectives.

例如：1. 他既会唱歌又会跳舞。
2. 坐地铁既方便又便宜。

我们来造句 • Make your own sentence

_____

（四）、不仅……而且……

"不仅……而且……"与"不但……而且……"的用法基本相同，但"不仅"还可以重叠成"不仅仅"在书面语中使用，使用的时候格式为"不仅仅是……"。

The patterns "不仅…而且…" and "不但…而且…" are basically used the same way. However, 不仅 can also appear as 不仅仅 in the written language, as in the pattern "不仅仅是…"

例如：1. 学汉语不仅要学说话，而且要学汉字。
2. 这不仅仅是你的事，也是我们大家的事。

我们来造句 • Make your own sentence

_____

五、汉语知识 • Chinese Knowledge

（一）、汉语的普通话 • Mandarin Chinese

汉语的普通话是"以北京语音为标准音，以北方话为基础方言、以典范的现代白话文著作为语法规范的现代汉民族共同语。"

普通话, or Mandarin Chinese, is based on a generalized northern accent, basic northern dialect, and the written 白话文 (or vernacular) as it appears in modern Chinese literature. It is the common language of the Han ethnicity.

（二）、汉语中的成语 • Chinese idioms

汉语中有一些固定格式的词语，其中以四个字的词语为最多，这些词语有一定的出处或典故，包含着很多中国传统的文化和历史。这些词语常用来表达固定的意思。因其字数少，但表达的意思很丰富，所以具有很强的表现力，恰当使用成语可以为文章增色，也可以体现一个人的汉语水平。课文中出现的"一言为定"、以及之前学过的"尊老爱幼"等都是成语。

Chinese has many fixed idiomatic expressions, among which four-character expressions are the most numerous. Such expressions have defined origins and background stories, including many Chinese traditions and historical accounts. Such expressions are known as 成语 and are used to express set ideas. Expressing rich meaning in relatively few characters, they are powerful means of expression and can make writing much more colorful. Their use can also reflect a person's mastery of Chinese. 一言为定 from this lesson and 尊老爱幼 from a previous lesson are both 成语.

六、相关链接，有关网络的词 • Related Terms: the Internet

1	网上视频	wǎngshàngshìpín	online video
2	网上购物	wǎngshànggòuwù	shopping online
3	电子邮件	diànzǐyóujiàn	e-mail
4	电子邮箱	diànzǐyóuxiāng	email address
5	网上下载	wǎngshàngxiàzǎi	download

七、文化生活小贴士 • Cultural Tips: Shenzhen introduction

（一）、深圳概况 • General introduction of Shenzhen

深圳与香港山水相连。在短短的30年里，深圳从一个小镇发展成为现代化国际化城市，创造了世界城市化、工业化和现代化的奇迹。深圳是中国口岸最多和惟一拥有海陆空口岸的城市，是中国与世界交往的主要门户之一，有着强劲的经济支撑与现代化的城市基础设施。深圳的城市综合竞争力位列内地城市第一。深圳将建设成为中国高新技术产业基地和区域性金融中心、信息中心、商贸中心、运输中心及旅游胜地，将成为现代化的国际性城市。到2010年8月26日深圳特区已经建立30周年了。2010年8月深圳成功举办了2011年第26届世界大学生运动会。

Shenzhen and Hong Kong are linked by mountains and rivers. In only 30 years, Shenzhen has developed from a small town into a modern city with international influences through miraculous urbanization, industrialization, and modernization. It has the most entry points of any city in mainland China, as well as mainland China's only open-sea port, making it an important gateway between China and the world. With a strong economy and modern infrastructure, it is mainland China's most economically competitive city.

In the future, Shenzhen will become China's base of high-technology manufacturing and a regional banking center. It will continue to develop as a center for information, trade, and transportation, and as a tourism destination. In the future, it will become a truly international city. August 26th, 2010, was the anniversary of Shenzhen's establishment as a Special Economic Zone. In 2011, it was host to the International University Sports Federation's 26th Universiade.

（二）、广东美食——早茶 • Cantonese delicacies - morning tea

广州人品茶大都一日早、中、晚三次，但早茶最为讲究，饮早茶的风气也最盛，由于饮早茶是喝茶的时候要配上点心，因此当地称饮早茶为吃早茶，实质是上酒楼"吃早餐"。泡上一壶茶，要上两件点心，美名"一盅两件"．早茶的品种很多，著名的有榴莲酥、叉烧包、凤爪、虾饺、马蹄糕、生滚鱼片粥、香芋卷、烧卖、龟苓膏、糯米鸡等等。

Cantonese people have tea times at three points in time during the day—in the morning, at noon, and in the evening. However, the morning tea is the one most worth mentioning and the one that remains a flourishing custom, largely because it is accompanied by various light snacks. Locally, drinking morning tea is referred to as "eating morning tea." It is, in fact, the same as having breakfast. Having a pot of tea with two different snacks is known as 一盅两件. There are many kinds of snacks served at morning tea. The most famous include durian pastries, barbecued pork buns, chicken feet, shrimp dumplings, chestnut noodles, fish congee, taro roll, steamed dumplings, herbal gelatin, and sticky rice in lotus leaves.

八、练习 • EXERCISES

（一）、填上合适的词语 • Fill in the blanks with appropriate words

回_____、_____　　　参观_____、_____

_____、_____狂　　　吸引_____、_____

购物_____、_____　　　一言_____

（二）、选词填空 • Fill in the blanks with the words provided

羡慕　好玩　决定　历史　发达　投资　风味　怀念

1. 如果想了解中国的_____，就要多看这方面的汉语书。
2. 欢乐谷有很多很_____的，很适合年轻人，但不适合老人。
3. 我喜欢各种_____的中国菜。
4. 他还没想好，所以不能作_____。
5. 深圳是个既年轻又_____的城市。
6. 回国以后他常_____在中国学习的日子。
7. 他不懂_____，所以赔了很多钱。
8. 她从不_____有钱人。

（三）、用所给词语完成句子 • Fill in the blanks with sentences using the words given in parentheses

1. A：这家饭馆的菜怎么样？
   B：_____。（既……又）

2. A：这个周末你打算做什么？
   B：_____。（另外）

3. A：你去过世界之窗吗？
   B：_____。（不仅……而且）

4. A：我们都去参观，你呢？
   B：_____ _____。（恐怕）

5. A：你的同学都是哪国人？
   B：_____。（来自）

6. A：你什么时候回国？
   B：_____。（决定）

7. A：来中国以后你的汉语怎么样？
   B：_____。（进步）

8. A：为什么学生都喜欢听他的课？
   B：_____。（吸引）

（四）、用所学词语表达 • Form sentences using the sentence patterns and words provided

▶ 听……这么说

1. 朋友说汉语很难学，你会怎么样？
2. 老师说考试很难，你会怎么样？
3. 朋友说深圳有很多购物广场，你会怎么样？
4. 朋友买了好吃的东西，请你去吃，你会怎么样？

▶ 别看……

1. 别看他看上去很年轻，_____。
2. 别看他汉语很好，_____。
3. 别看他不戴眼镜，_____。
4. 别看这道菜只有两种东西，_____。

▶ 想……什么都有

1. 书店有各种各样的书，_____。
2. 饭馆有各种风味的菜，_____。
3. 娱乐场所有各种好玩的，_____。
4. 家里有很多DVD，_____。

▶ 恐怕

1. 回家太晚，_____。
2. 时间太短，_____。
3. 天气不好，_____。
4. 有急事儿，_____。

（五）、词语连线 • Match words to form short phrases

移民　　上网　　吸引　　风味　　参观　　全国　　怀念　　逛

客人　　城市　　餐厅　　景点　　街　　各地　　聊天　　朋友

（六）、解释下列句中"好"字的意思和用法

Explain the meaning of 好 in the following sentences

1. 你**好**！
2. 他的汉语很**好**。
3. 这件衣服很**好**看。
4. 中国菜很**好**吃。
5. 请准备**好**零钱。
6. 我们一起去**好**吗？
7. 欢乐谷有很多**好**玩儿的东西。
8. 吃哪种药**好**得快？

（七）、你了解深圳的历史吗？在网上找一些有关深圳的故事讲给大家听

Are you familiar with the history of Shenzhen? Search online for stories about Shenzhen and share with the class.

（八）、请你向朋友介绍一下儿深圳的旅游景点、美食、购物、风俗习惯等等。你去过下面的哪个旅游景点？谈谈对它的印象

Tell the class about Shenzhen's tourist attractions, cuisine, shopping, and customs. To which of the following sites have you gone? What impressions do you have of them?

锦绣中华　　世界之窗　　欢乐谷　　华强北　　万象城

（九）、来聊天吧 • Discuss

1. 深圳最吸引你的地方是什么？

   What about Shenzhen most attracted you?

2. 你游览过深圳的哪些景点？你最喜欢哪个地方？

   What places have you been to in Shenzhen? Which ones do you like best?

3. 介绍一下儿你居住的城市。

   Tell about a city in which you previously lived.

第十二课 / LESSON 12

路上辛苦了!
YOUR TRIP HERE WAS STRENUOUS!

这一课我们将学到 • In this lesson we will study the following:
1. 与去机场接人有关的内容
2. 重点词语：糟糕、就要……了、……，不然……、再说、认不出、还不……、倒、难道、吃醋、小心眼儿、算账
3. 汉语知识：汉语中的典故

一、课文 • Text

（去深圳宝安机场的路上 • On the way to the Bao'an airport）

 司机： 前面好像塞车啦，恐怕要等很久啊！
Ahead it seems traffic is blocked. I'm afraid we'll have to wait a long time.

 吴帅： 是发生交通事故了吗？
Is it because a traffic accident has occurred?

 司机： 好像是吧。
It seems it is.

 吴帅： 真糟糕！怎么办？
Really rotten! How do we deal with this?

 司机： 没办法，只好等。
There's no way to deal with it. We're forced to wait.

终于到了机场 • They finally arrive at the airport

 艾美丽： 现在几点了？
What time is it now?

 吴帅： 两点了，美善坐的飞机几点到？
It's just turned 2:00. What time does Mei Shan's flight arrive?

	艾美丽：	她坐的飞机是两点十分（到），一会儿要到了。还好，我们没有迟到。 Her flight arrives at 2:10. A little while, and it will arrive. It's still OK. We aren't late.
	吴帅：	我们得快点儿，不然，就来不及了。 We have to go faster. Otherwise, there isn't enough time.
	艾美丽：	不用着急，她下飞机后还得取行李，再说，她见不到我们她会给我们打电话的。 We don't need to worry. After she's gotten off the plane, she still has to get her luggage. Additionally, if she doesn't see us, she can give us a telephone call.
	吴帅：	哎，你看大屏幕，她坐的那次航班晚点了，晚了半小时。 Ai! Look at the big screen. Her flight is late. It's late by half an hour.
	艾美丽：	那她应该是两点四十分到。 Then she should arrive at 2:40.
	吴帅：	这样的话我们就不用着急了，我们慢慢儿走就行了。 If it's this way, we don't need to worry. We can slowly walk there, and it's OK

吴帅和艾美丽在旅客出口处等 • Wu Shuai and Emily are waiting at the exit

	吴帅：	时间差不多了，应该到了。 It's just about time. She should have arrived.
	艾美丽：	我和美善很长时间没见面了，她不会认不出我了吧？ I and Mei Shan haven't seen each other for a long time. She can't not recognize me, right?
	吴帅：	欸，你看，那个女孩儿在向你挥手，是不是美善？ Hey, look! That young woman waving toward you, is that Mei Shan
	艾美丽：	是啊，就是她，就是美善。 It is. That is her. That is Mei Shan.

吴帅和艾美丽接到了美善 • Wu Shuai and Emily have picked up Mei Shan

	美善：	我们又见面了，好想你啊！ We meet again. I've really missed you.
	艾美丽：	是啊，我太高兴了！ Yes. I am too happy now.
	美善：	这位是……？还不快介绍介绍。 This person is …? Hurry up and introduce us.

艾美丽： 对、对、对！我光顾高兴了，忘了介绍。他是我男朋友吴帅，这位是我好朋友美善。
Right, right, right. I'm only concentrating on being happy and forgot to introduce you. He is my boyfriend, Wu Shuai. This person is my friend, Mei Shan.

吴帅： 你好，美善，欢迎来到深圳，路上辛苦了！
Hello, Mei Shan. Welcome to Shenzhen. Your trip here was strenuous.

美善： 你好，吴帅！很高兴认识你！怎么是"无帅"？应该是"很帅"！
Hello, Wu Shuai. I'm very happy to meet you. How is your name "Not Handsome"? It should be "Very Handsome".

吴帅： 谢谢夸奖！你和你的名字倒是很配，又美丽又善良。
Thanks for the empty flattery! You and your name, on the other hand, are very well matched. You're both beautiful and kind-hearted.

艾美丽： 吴帅，你这么说，难道不怕我吃醋吗？
Wu Shuai, you talk like this, and you aren't afraid I'll get jealous?

吴帅： 不会吧，我知道你没有那么小心眼儿！
You can't be, right? I know you don't have that petty a personality.

艾美丽： 车来了，我们先上车吧，回去再跟你算账！
A car is coming. First we'll get in, OK? Once we're going back, I'll settle accounts with you!

二、根据课文回答问题 · ANSWER THE FOLLOWING QUESTIONS ACCORDING TO THE TEXT

1. 艾美丽和吴帅接美善的路上为什么塞车了？
　　_____

2. 艾美丽他们迟到了吗？
　　_____

3. 美善坐的航班晚了多长时间？
　　_____

4. 美善以前见过吴帅吗？
　　_____

5. 美善觉得吴帅怎么样？
　　_____

6. 吴帅担心艾美丽吃醋吗？
　　_____

三、生词 • Vocabulary

1	辛苦	xīnkǔ	形、动	strenuous, hard, difficult
2	发生	fāshēng	动	to happen, to occur
3	交通	jiāotōng	名	traffic
4	事故	shìgù	名	accident
5	糟糕	zāogāo	形	bad, terrible, rotten [literally, "rotten cake"]
6	办	bàn	动	to handle, to manage, to deal with
7	办法	bànfǎ	名	method, means, way
8	只好	zhǐhǎo	副	have to, be forced to
9	终于	zhōngyú	副	finally
10	飞机	fēijī	名	airplane
11	就要……了	jiùyào……le		[see Word Usage]
12	还好	háihǎo		not bad, still good
13	得	děi	助动	have to, should, must
14	不然	bùrán		otherwise
15	来不及	láibují		not have enough time
16	不用	búyòng		need not, don't need to
17	再说	zàishuō		in addition, moreover, besides
18	屏幕	píngmù	名	screen
19	航班	hángbān	名	flight
20	晚点	wǎndiǎn		late, behind schedule
21	……的话	……dehuà		in the event that…
22	旅客	lǚkè	名	tourist, traveler
23	出口	chūkǒu	名	exit
24	认	rèn	动	to recognize
25	女孩儿	nǚháir	名	girl, young woman
26	向	xiàng	介	in the direction of, towards
27	挥	huī	动	to wave
28	手	shǒu	名	hand
29	顾	gù	动	to attend to, to pay attention to, to care for
30	认识	rènshi	动	to recognize, to know
31	无	wú	动、副	to lack, not to have; without, lacking
32	帅	shuài	形	handsome
33	夸奖	kuājiǎng	动	to praise, to flatter
34	倒	dào	副	on the other hand, in contrast
35	配	pèi	动、形	to set off, to match; complementary
36	善良	shànliáng	形	kind-hearted
37	难道	nándào	副	[see Word Usage]

38	醋	cù	名	vinegar
39	吃醋	chīcù		to be jealous
40	心眼儿	xīnyǎnr		heart, mind, intelligence
41	算	suàn	动	to calculate, to settle
42	账	zhàng	名	account
43	算账	suànzhàng		to criticize, to scold, to settle accounts

四、词语解释 • Word Usage

(一)、糟糕!

汉语中,"糟糕"的意思是出现了很坏的情况。可修饰名词,也常在口语中用作插入语或独立成句。

糟糕 is used to indicate a bad situation has occurred. It can modify nouns. It can also be used as a parenthetical expression or to stand alone as a sentence in speech.

例如: 1. 糟糕!我的钱包不见了。
2. 糟糕!来不及了,要迟到了。
3. A: 外面下大雨了!
   B: 糟糕!

我们来造句 • Make your own sentence

_____

(二)、就要……了

汉语中,"就要……了"的意思是表示很快会做某事或出现某种情况。其中"要"是"将要"的意思,常和"就"、"快"一起用,组成"就要……了"、"快要……了",增强"快"、"马上"的意思。至于两者的区别我们将在后面讲到。

The pattern "就要…了" indicates an event will occur soon. Here, 要 has the same meaning as 将要. It is often used with 就 or 快 in the patterns "就要…了" and "快要…了" to emphasize immediacy. The differences between these patterns will be discussed later.

例如: 1. 就要考试了,我不能跟你去玩儿了。
2. 就要吃饭了,你别吃巧克力了。

我们来造句 • Make your own sentence

_____

(三)、……,不然……

在这里,"不然"的意思是"如果不这样"。一般出现在后一个小句子中,表示不"这样"的后果或结论,而前一个小句子中的内容是说"应该这样"。常在后面加上"的话",强调假设的语气。

Here, 不然 has the same meaning as 如果不这样. It is usually preceded by a clause stating a condition or situation that should occur. 不然 then appears at the beginning of a second clause which describes a result of the previously stated condition or situation's not occurring. It is also often followed by 的话 (3), which adds emphasis.

例如： 1. 你快走吧，不然来不及了。
2. 你要多跟中国人聊天，不然你的汉语进步很慢。
3. 你快告诉他吧，不然的话，他会生气的。

我们来造句 • Make your own sentence

___

（四）、……，再说，……

在这里，"再说"是承接前面的小句，引出后面的小句，补充前面小句中的原因、条件、情况等等。"再说"不能用于前面小句中，也不能单独使用。

Here, 再说 is used to carry on from an earlier clause and introduce another clause. It introduces an addition, such as a cause, requirement, or situation. It cannot be used in an initial clause and cannot stand alone as a sentence.

例如： 1. 我不想去韩国了，因为我没时间，再说，我也没有钱。
2. 我不买这件衣服了，我穿有点儿大，再说，也太贵了。
3. 我不想参加考试了，我还没复习好，再说，现在报名也来不及了。

我们来造句 • Make your own sentence

___

（五）、她不会认不出我了吧？

在这里，"出"表示动作的结果，也用"出来"表示。意思是表示人或事物随着主要动词的动作而明显、突出或明了。"认不出"的意思是，"看见了但却不知道是谁或什么"。肯定形式是"认得出"。类似的词语还有"猜得出（来）"、"猜不出（来）"、"看得出"、"看不出"等等。

Here, 出 is a directional verb. It can also be written 出来. It indicates that a person or thing cannot perform an action with a clear result. 认不出 means that a person sees someone or something without being able to clearly recognize who or what it is. The affirmative form is 认得出. Other such forms include 猜得出, 猜不出, 看得出, and 看不出.

例如： 1. A：这是什么？
B：我看不出来。
2. A：你猜，这是谁的？
B：我猜不出来。

我们来造句 • Make your own sentence

_____

（六）、<u>还不</u>快给我介绍介绍

在这里"还不……"表示应该做什么或希望某种情况发生。加上"快"是表示催促某人做某事的意思。

Here, 还不 indicates that an action should be performed or that a situation should occur. Adding 快 indicates a demand or request that an action be performed quickly.

    例如：1. 你还不写作业！
       2. 怎么还不下雨？太热了！
       3. 他还不来？
       4. 你还不快来！
       5. 你还不快复习，明天就要考试了！

我们来造句 • Make your own sentence

_____

（七）、你和你的名字<u>倒</u>是很配

在这里，"倒"是副词，表示强调语气，强调相反的意思。

Here 倒 is an adverb used for emphasis. Emphasis is placed on a contrast or reversal.

    例如：1. 这件事情我不知道，他倒知道。
       2. 今天出来得很早，倒迟到了。

我们来造句 • Make your own sentence

_____

（八）、难道

汉语中，"难道"的意思是加强反问的语气。可用在动词前，也可用在主语前，句尾常接"吗"，形成"难道……吗"的格式。

难道 emphasizes a rhetorical question. It can be used before a verb or in front of a subject. 吗 is added to the end of the sentence to complete the pattern "难道…吗?"

    例如：1. 你难道不知道吗？（意思是：你应该知道。）
       2. 难道你没听见我说的话吗？（意思是：你应该听见了）
       3. 难道这样不行吗？（意思是：我觉得这样行）

我们来造句 • Make your own sentence

_____

（九）、吃醋

在这里，"吃醋"的意思是嫉妒。"吃醋"是动宾结构的词语，如果有嫉妒的对象，表达的方式是"吃……的醋"。

Here, 吃醋 means to experience jealousy or envy. It is a verb-object verb. If there is a direct object, it is placed after 吃, and then followed by 的醋 (2).

例如： 1. 她一看见男朋友跟别的女孩子在一起就吃醋。
2. 我这么漂亮，怎么会吃她的醋？

我们来造句 • Make your own sentence

（十）、小心眼儿

汉语中，"小心眼儿"的意思是表示一个人心胸狭窄，计较小事、容易为小事不高兴。在使用时，相当于一个形容词。

小心眼儿 indicates that a person is narrow-minded, quick to argue about petty concerns, or becomes upset over small problems. In usage, the expression corresponds to an adjective.

例如： 1. 她什么都好，就是有点儿小心眼儿。
2. 他不是小心眼儿的人，不会生气的。
3. 你太小心眼儿了！

我们来造句 • Make your own sentence

（十一）、回去再跟你<u>算账</u>！

在这里，"算账"是惩罚、批评、责骂的意思。"算账"是动宾结构的词语，不能直接带宾语。一般用"跟"把宾语提前，形成"跟……算账"的格式。有时也说"找……算账"。

Here, 算账 means to scold, to punish, or to criticize. It is a verb-object verb and cannot be followed by a direct object. Usually, 跟 is used to move direct objects before the verb, according to the pattern "跟…算账." The pattern "和…算账" can also be used.

例如： 1. 今天我没时间了，明天再跟你算账。
2. 这是他的错，你不应该跟我说，你应该跟他算账去。

我们来造句 • Make your own sentence

五、汉语知识 • Chinese Knowledge

汉语中的"典故" • Chinese "allusions"

汉语的历史悠久,古代书中有很多故事或传说,常被后人引用、流传,并用简洁的词语固定下来,成为"典故"。人们在写文章或说话时,喜欢引用典故,这样可以使文章或说话的内容变得既丰富又生动。学习一些典故不仅可以提高汉语水平,还可以通过学习典故了解中国的历史和文化。课文中的"吃醋"就是一个典故。

传说,唐朝的一个皇帝要赐给一位大臣几名美女做妾,大臣因为怕老婆不敢接受,皇帝就派人带着一壶"毒酒"去找大臣的老婆,说如果不接受这几名美妾,就请她喝了毒酒。大臣的老婆,把"毒酒"喝了,结果却没死。原来壶中装的是醋,皇帝是用这个方法来考验她。后来人们就用"吃醋"来表示嫉妒的意思。

Chinese has a long history. Historical records include many stories and legends that later people quoted, retold, and from which many simple, fixed terms eventually descended. Such terms are known as 典故, or allusions. When writing or speaking, most people like to use such allusions to make their writing and conversation more meaningful and vivid. Studying allusions can help improve students' Chinese levels, as well as help them better understand China's history and culture.

吃醋 is one such allusion. According to legend, a Tang dynasty emperor wished to give a minister several beautiful women as concubines. The minister, though, was worried that his wife might not accept such an arrangement. The emperor sent people to take a container of poison to the minister's wife and tell her that, if she would not accept her husband's concubines, then she should drink the poison.

The minister's wife drank the poison, yet she did not die. In truth, the container held only vinegar, not poison, and the emperor had only used this deceit to test her feelings. After that, 吃醋 became used to indicate jealousy.

六、相关链接,汉语中常用的客套话 • COMMONLY USED POLITE EXPRESSIONS

1	劳驾	láo//jià	"May I trouble you?"
2	借光	jiè//guāng	"Excuse me."
3	告辞	gào//cí	to say goodbye, to take leave
4	请教	qǐngjiào	to ask for advice or an opinion
5	恭喜	gōngxǐ	"Congratulations!"

七、文化生活小贴士 • CULTURAL TIPS: MORE POLITE EXPRESSIONS

汉语中的客套话 • More polite expressions

初次见面说"久仰"； 好久不见说"久违"； 等候客人用"恭候"； 宾客来到称"光临"；
未及欢迎说"失迎"； 起身作别称"告辞"； 看望别人说"拜访"； 请人别送用"留步"；
陪伴朋友用"奉陪"； 中途告辞用"失陪"； 请人原谅说"包涵"； 请人批评说"指教"；
求人解答用"请教"； 盼人指点用"赐教"； 欢迎购买说"惠顾"； 请人受礼称"笑纳"；
请人帮助说"劳驾"； 求给方便说"借光"； 麻烦别人说"打扰"； 托人办事用"拜托"；
向人祝贺说"恭喜"； 赞人见解称"高见"； 对方来信称"惠书"； 赠人书画题"惠存"；
尊称老师为"恩师"； 称人学生为"高足"； 请人休息说"节劳"； 对方不适说"欠安"；
老人年龄说"高寿"； 女士年龄称"芳龄"； 平辈年龄问"贵庚"； 打听姓名问"贵姓"；
称人夫妇为"伉俪"； 称人女儿为"千金"。

八、练习 • EXERCISES

（一）、填上合适的词语 • Fill in the blanks with appropriate words

吃_____、_____　　算_____、_____
挥_____、_____　　航班_____、_____
发生_____、_____

（二）、选词填空 • Fill in the blanks with the words provided

事故　晚点　介绍　夸奖　善良　终于　配　办法

1. 大家_____他汉语说得好。
2. 她不但长得漂亮，而且非常_____。
3. 出门的时候碰到了交通_____，所以迟到了。
4. 大屏幕上写着_____航班的航班号。
5. 我觉得他们俩很_____。
6. 他等了很长时间，_____等来了一辆出租车。
7. 我给你_____一下儿，这位是王老师。
8. 这个_____很好，我也试一试。

（三）、用所给词语完成句子

Fill in the blanks with sentences using the words given in parentheses

1. A：我今天有事，不能跟你一起去听音乐会了。
   B：_____。（只好）
2. A：我来你都不知道。

B: _____。（光顾）

3. A：你最近身体怎么样？

   B: _____。（糟糕）

4. A：你现在习惯吃中国菜了吗？

   B: _____。（还好）

5. A：你为什么不跟朋友去欢乐谷？

   B: _____。（再说）

6. A：小王好像生气了？

   B: _____。（吃醋）

7. A：我打电话的时候你做什么呢？

   B: _____。（在）

8. A：是我错了，但大家都在，先别说了。

   B: _____。（算账）

（四）、用所学词语表达 • Form sentences using the sentence patterns and words provided

▶ ……的话

1. 告诉朋友来深圳时，你去接。
2. 告诉朋友身体不好，要休息。
3. 告诉同学有问题问老师。
4. 担心堵车会迟到。

▶ 不然

1. 你要好好休息，_____。
2. 你一定要来，_____。
3. 下雨了，要带伞，_____。
4. 不要喝那么多酒，_____。

▶ 还不快……

1. 要迟到了，_____。
2. 发烧了，_____。
3. 明天有考试，_____。
4. 头发太长了，_____。

（五）、用所学词语改写句子 • Rewrite the sentences using the words provided

▶ 就要……了

1. 秋天快过去了，天气慢慢地冷了。　　_____
2. 情人节来了，买支玫瑰花给女朋友。　　_____
3. 台风来了，把衣服收起来。　　_____

4. 老师来了，准备上课。 _____

▶ 难道

1. 你应该知道这件事。 _____
2. 你喜欢这首歌。 _____
3. 你们不认识。 _____
4. 不相信你的话是真的。 _____

▶ 倒

1. 今天没带雨伞，下雨了。 _____
2. 他不是四川人，比四川人喜欢吃辣的。 _____
3. 平时不堵车，星期天堵车。 _____
4. 考试没准备，考得好。 _____

▶ 得

1. 我应该早点儿休息。 _____
2. 朋友来了，要去机场接。 _____
3. 感冒了，要去医院看病。 _____
4. 在家请客，要去超市买菜。 _____

（六）、词语连线 • Match words to form short phrases

菜很多　　很久没过面　　时间太短了　　天很黑　　忘了东西在哪儿

来不及　　认不出　　吃不完　　找不到　　看不见

（七）、用所给的词语介绍一个人 • Use the words provided to introduce someone

心眼儿　　善良　　吃醋　　帅　　夸奖

（八）、角色扮演 • Performance

A同学扮演主人，去机场接B同学到饭店用餐。

Student A plays a host and goes to the airport to pick up Student B and take Student B to a restaurant.

（九）、来聊天吧 • Discuss

1. 你觉得深圳的交通怎么样？你经历（jīnglì, experience）过很糟糕的事情吗？谈谈你的感受？ What is your opinion of the traffic in Shenzhen? Have you experienced any negative situations? Tell about your experiences.

2. 如果你是深圳市市长，你会怎么改善深圳的交通？
If you were mayor of Shenzhen, what would you do to improve Shenzhen's traffic?

第十三课 / LESSON 13
我想在深圳找工作
I WANT TO FIND WORK IN SHENZHEN

这一课我们将学到 • In this lesson we will study the following:
1. 与找工作有关的内容
2. 重点词语：跟……有关、是否
3. 汉语知识：汉语中的"口语"和"书面语"

一、课文 • Text

 艾美丽：
美善，你这次来深圳是想继续学汉语吗？
Mei Shan, did you come to Shenzhen this time wanting to continue studying Chinese?

 美善：
我想在深圳找工作。
I want to find work in Shenzhen.

 吴帅：
你想找什么样的工作？
What type of work do you want to find?

 美善：
我想找一份跟经济管理有关的工作。
I want to find a job related to economic management.

 吴帅：
我朋友的公司正在招聘财政主管，你要不要试一下儿？
My friend's company is currently recruiting a financial director. Do you want to interview or not?

 美善：
好啊！你能给我推荐一下儿吗？
Great. Could you recommend me?

 吴帅：
那我打电话问一下儿吧。（吴帅拿出朋友的名片，拨通电话）
Then I'll make a telephone call and ask, OK? (Wu Shuai takes out his friend's name card and dials)

 张强：
喂！
Hi!

吴帅: 张强，你好！我是吴帅，你不是要找一位财政主管吗？我给你推荐一位怎么样？

张强: 谁啊？

吴帅: 你等一下儿，我让她自己跟你讲好吗？

张强: 好吧。

吴帅把电话给美善 • Wu Shuai gives the phone to Mei Shan

美善: 张总，你好！我是吴帅的朋友。

张强: 你好！请简单介绍一下儿你自己好吗？

美善: 我叫金美善，是韩国人，我1999年从美国长岛大学本科毕业，取得经济学学士学位。

张强: 我们提供的岗位是公司财政主管，你能胜任吗？

美善: 我相信我可以。大学毕业后，2003年至2007年，我在一家石油公司做过财政主管，所以我有这方面的经验和能力。

张强: 你期待的薪金是多少？

美善: 平均月收入一万元。

张强: 好的，我现在还不能决定是否可以录用你，请你星期一来我的公司面试，同时你也可以看一下儿我们这儿的工作环境。

美善: 好的，谢谢，星期一见！

张强： 再见！
See you again.

美善： （美善放下电话）吴帅，太谢谢你了！
(Mei Shan hangs up the phone) Wu Shuai, thank you so much.

吴帅： 别客气！你当上主管以后别忘了请我们吃饭哟！
Don't mention it. After you've started work as director, don't forget to treat us to dinner.

美善： 没问题！
No problem.

二、根据课文回答问题 · Answer the following questions according to the text

1. 美善来深圳是想继续学汉语吗？
　　_____

2. 美善想找什么样的工作？
　　_____

3. 美善哪年从美国哪个大学本科毕业，取得了什么学位？
　　_____

4. 美善在一家石油公司做过什么工作？
　　_____

5. 美善期待的薪金是多少？
　　_____

三、生词 · Vocabulary

1	继续	jìxù	动	to continue
2	份	fèn	量	[a measure word, for a work position]
3	跟……有关	gēn……yǒuguān		to be related to…
4	经济	jīngjì	名	economy, economics, finance
5	招聘	zhāopìn	动	to recruit, to advertise for workers
6	财政	cáizhèng	名	finance
7	主管	zhǔguǎn	名	person in charge, director
8	推荐	tuījiàn	动	to recommend
9	名片	míngpiàn	名	name card, business card
10	拨	bō	动	to dial, to enter a number
11	通	tōng	动	to connect, to open up

12	自己	zìjǐ	代	oneself
13	总（经理）	zǒng（jīnglǐ）	名	general (manager)
14	简单	jiǎndān	形	simple
15	本科	běnkē	名	undergraduate
16	毕业	bìyè	动、名	to graduate; graduation
17	取得	qǔdé	动	to get, to take
18	……学	……xué	名	field of study
19	学士	xuéshì	名	Bachelor's, undergraduate
20	学位	xuéwèi	名	academic degree
21	提供	tígōng	动	to provide
22	岗位	gǎngwèi	名	work position
23	胜任	shèngrèn	动	to be competent for, to be qualified for
24	至	zhì	动	to, until
25	石油	shíyóu	名	petroleum, oil
26	经验	jīngyàn	名	experience
27	能力	nénglì	名	capability, ability
28	期待	qīdài	动、名	to expect; expectation
29	薪金	xīnjīn	名	salary, recompense
30	平均	píngjūn	形、动	on average; to distribute evenly
31	收入	shōurù	名	salary, remuneration
32	万	wàn	数	ten thousand
33	是否	shìfǒu		whether, whether or not
34	录用	lùyòng	动	to employ, to recruit
35	放	fàng	动	to release, to stop
36	当	dāng	动	to work as, to act as, to be
37	哟	yo	助	[particle: placed at the end of a sentence to indicate an imperative]

专名词 • Proper Names

38	张强	zhāngqiáng	Zhang Qiang
39	美国长岛大学	měiguózhángdǎodàxué	Long Island University

四、词语解释 • Word Usage

（一）、跟……有关

在这里，"跟"是表示事物之间的某种关系，"关"是"关系"的意思，"跟……有关"是"跟……有关系"的意思，也可用"与……有关"、"和……有关"。否定形式是"跟……（无关）没关系"、"和……没关系"。"与……无关"常用于书面语。

Here, 跟 indicates a relationship between two nouns. 关 has the same meaning as 关系. The patterns "与…有关" and "和…有关" are also commonly used. The negative forms are "跟…没有关系" and "与…无关." "与…无关" is used in written language.

例如：1. 他经常看一些跟历史有关的书。
2. 这件事跟你有关吗？
3. 专业人士认为这种病与环境无关，与生活习惯有关。
4. 你别跟我说，这件事和我没关系。

我们来造句 • Make your own sentence

___

（二）、是否

"是否"的意思是"是不是"，常用于书面语。

是否 has the same meaning as 是不是. It is usually used in written language.

例如：1. 请问，我是否可以向您提一个问题？
2. 填写简历的时候要写清楚你是否有在国外留学的经历。

我们来造句 • Make your own sentence

___

五、汉语知识 • Chinese Knowledge

汉语中的"口语"和"书面语" • Speech versus written language

汉语中的"口语"是指人们在平时交流的时候使用的语言，书面语是指书写在文本中的或是在正式场合以及交流双方不太熟悉、表示客气的时候使用的语言。同一种事物，"口语"和"书面语"所使用的词语是不同的。例如："妈妈"和"母亲"，"没关系"和"无关"，"是不是"和"是否"等等。其中"妈妈"、"没关系"、"是不是"是口语的表达方式，"母亲"、"无关"、"是否"则是书面语。

In Chinese, 口语, or "speech," refers to the language used in everyday conversation. 书面语, or "written language" refers not only to the language used in writing, but also to the language generally spoken during formal occasions or when people speak to someone with whom they are not well-acquainted. 书面语 has a polite tone. 口语 and 书面语 often express the same idea using very different terms. For example, the terms 妈妈, 没关系 and 是不是 are all "speech" terms, while the "written language" terms are, respectively, 母亲, 无关, and 是否.

六、相关链接 • Related Terms: employment

（一）、与应聘有关的词语 • Words related to employment

| 1 | 简历 | jiǎnlì | résumé, CV |

2	健康状况	jiànkāngzhuàngkuàng	physical condition
3	学历	xuélì	record of education, educational background
4	硕士	shuòshì	Master's degree
5	邮箱	yóuxiāng	mailbox
6	邮政编码	yóuzhèngbiānmǎ	postal code, zip code
7	地址	dìzhǐ	address
8	经历	jīnglì	experience
9	专栏作家	zhuānlánzuòjiā	columnist
10	意向	yìxiàng	intention, purpose
11	待遇	dàiyù	salary, wages and benefits
12	面试官	miànshìguān	interviewer
13	应聘者	yìngpìnzhě	job applicant
14	教育背景	jiàoyùbèijǐng	educational background
15	教育学	jiàoyùxué	education, pedagogy
16	心理学	xīnlǐxué	psychology
17	通知	tōngzhī	announcement
18	应聘	yìngpìn	to accept an offer of employment
19	经理	jīnglǐ	manager
20	求职信	qiúzhíxìn	application letter
21	工作经历	gōngzuòjīnglì	work experience

（二）、个人简历样本 • Sample résumé

个 人 基 本 资 料				
姓　名	艾美丽	性别	女	照片
出生地	美国	出生年月	1978.5	
计算机能力	中级	语言能力	英语（熟练） 汉语（HSK高级）	
健康状况	良好	所学专业	经济与贸易 教育学	
毕业学校	长岛大学 1995-1999 深圳大学 2005-2010	学历	本科学士学位 硕士在读	
联系电话	0755-83266688	手机	15829107810	
邮政编码	518060	邮箱e-mail	aimeili@gmail.com	
通信地址	深圳大学留学生楼			
工作经历				
2007-2010 对外英语教师 2003-2007 外企财政主管 2000-2003 纽约杂志经济专栏作家				
求职意向		待遇要求		
岗位类型：经济管理 工作地区：上海、浙江		一万/月，可面议		

七、文化生活小贴士 • Tips for Daily Life: Shenzhen jobs

1. Job592.com 深圳留学生创业园 Employment information from the Shenzhen Overseas Chinese High-tech Venture Park can be found at job592.com.
2. 深圳国际人才网留学生联谊会 talents.sz.gov.cn/lyh/ is the website for the Shenzhen International Talent Network Student Association.

八、练习 • Exercises

（一）、填上合适的词语 • Fill in the blanks with appropriate words

当_____、_____　　　_____、_____学

_____、_____管理　　　提供_____、_____

（二）、选词填空 • Fill in the blanks with the words provided

继续　　招聘　　推荐　　胜任　　能力　　是否　　经济　　简单

1. 听说一家外国公司正在_____大学毕业生，我想去试试。
2. 大家都_____小王当经理。
3. 您_____能介绍一下儿这个城市的历史？
4. 我听说这次考试非常_____，你不用担心。
5. 深圳是个_____发达的城市。
6. 听说他家里发生了一些事，不知他是否能_____学习。
7. 他虽然人很好，但_____不强。
8. 他经验丰富，我相信他能_____这个工作。

（三）、用所给的词语完成句子

Fill in the blanks with sentences using the words given in parentheses.

1. A：他为什么生气了？
   B：_____。（跟……有关）
2. A：_____？（是否）
   B：当然可以。
3. A：你知道小王为什么不喜欢我吗？
   B：_____。（让）
4. A：你以前做什么工作？
   B：_____。（当）
5. A：你平时经常去逛街吗？
   B：_____。（平均）

（四）、词语连线 • Match words to form short phrases

经济　　学士　　拨通　　提供　　本科　　经验

毕业　　学位　　岗位　　管理　　电话　　丰富

（五）、使用划线词语仿造例句造句 • Use the underlined words to form sentences

1. 我2005年**至**2009年在中国学汉语

   _____

2. 你**是否**喜欢打网球？

   _____

3. 这件事**跟**小王**有关**。

   _____

（六）、模仿课文，写一份简历

Using the sample as a model, write your own résumé.

（七）、角色扮演 • Performance

两位同学分别扮演面试官和应聘者进行会话练习。

Students work in pairs. One plays an interviewer, and the other plays a candidate. Prepare a conversation.

（八）、根据对联猜职业 • Guess what occupations the following couplets describe

1. 做天下头等事业，用世间顶上功夫。
2. 一把曲尺，能成方圆器，几根直线，造就栋梁材。
3. 虽住两间火烤烟熏屋，却是一位千锤百炼人。

（九）、来聊天吧 • Discuss

1. 来中国前你工作过吗？讲讲你求职的经历。

   Before coming to China, had you worked? Talk about your experiences looking for work.

2. 在你的国家什么职业比较受欢迎？为什么？

   What occupations are most desirable in your home country? Why?

第十四课 / LESSON 14

带什么礼物回国好?
WHAT PRESENTS ARE GOOD TO TAKE BACK TO MY COUNTRY?

这一课我们将学到 • In this lesson we will study the following:
1. 与送礼物有关的内容
2. 重点词语:要……了、快……了、除了……还……、这样吧
3. 辨析:"快……了"、"快要……了"、"就要……了"和"要……了"、"或者"和"还是"
4. 汉语知识:"动词+的"意义和用法

一、课文 • Text

(艾美丽要回国了,和同学们商量带什么礼物回国 • Emily is returning to her home country. She is talking with classmates about what presents to take back)

 艾美丽:
快放假了,我要回国看我的家人和朋友,你们觉得带什么礼物回去好呢?
Soon, we have a vacation. I will go back to my country and visit my family and friends. What do you think? What presents are good to take back to my country?

 艾美丽的同学:
那可多啦。吃的、穿的、钱包、杯子,这些都可以。
There are so many—food, clothing, purses. These are all OK.

 艾美丽:
嗯,不好吧,太普通了。想些特别点儿的,或者他们需要的。
Umm, no good. Those are too common. Think of something special, or of something they'd need.

 艾美丽的同学:
他们有什么爱好吗?
What hobbies do they have?

 艾美丽:
很多,比如看书,养花,还有旅游。
Very many, for example, reading, growing flowers, also traveling.

 艾美丽的同学:
那你可以送一些跟养花和旅游有关的书。
Then you can give them some books about growing flowers and traveling.

	艾美丽：	嗯，我想送她们既实用又有中国特色的东西。 Umm, I want to give them something both useful and having Chinese characteristics.
	艾美丽：	中国的茶非常有名，你可以带些茶回去，而且茶很轻，好带。 China's tea is very famous. You can take some tea back. Additionally, tea is very light. It's easy to carry.
	艾美丽：	除了茶还有什么？ Outside of tea, what else is there?
	艾美丽：	你可以买些工艺品，像扇子、中国结、剪纸、泥人、脸谱等等。 You can buy some arts and crafts, like fans, Chinese knots, paper-cuttings, clay figurines, painted masks, and so on.
	艾美丽：	好主意。另外，我爸爸很喜欢中国画，你们知道哪儿卖画吗？ Good ideas. Aside from those, my father likes Chinese paintings. Do you know where they sell paintings?
	艾美丽的同学：	大芬村。那里是闻名世界的"油画村"。 Dafen Cun. That is a world-renowned "Oil painting village."
	吴帅：	这样吧，我送你一幅。是我爷爷画的，他是个画家。算是我送给你的回国礼物吧。 Or this way, right? I'll give you one. It's one my grandfather painted. He's a painter. Consider it as me giving you a going-home present, OK?
	艾美丽：	那太谢谢你了。 Then, thank you so much.

二、根据课文回答问题 • ANSWER THE FOLLOWING QUESTIONS ACCORDING TO THE TEXT

1. 艾美丽为什么要和同学们商量买礼物的事？
   _____

2. 艾美丽觉得吃的、穿的、钱包、杯子这些礼物怎么样？
   _____

3. 艾美丽想送家人和朋友什么礼物？
   _____

4. 艾美丽的同学为什么建议艾美丽带茶叶？
   _____

5. 课文中提到了哪些中国特色的工艺品？
   _____

6. 艾美丽的同学送给艾美丽一件什么礼物，为什么？这件礼物是买的吗？
   _____

三、生词 • Vocabulary

1	礼物	lǐwù	名	gift, present
2	要……了	yào……le		[see Word Usage and Distinguish]
3	快……了	kuài……le		[see Word Usage and Distinguish]
4	假	jià	名	holiday, vacation
5	放假	fàng//jià	(动宾)动	to have a holiday, to have a vacation
6	看（望）	kàn（wàng）	动	to visit
7	家人	jiārén	名	family
8	钱包	qiánbāo	名	purse, wallet
9	杯子	bēizi	名	cup, glass
10	或者	huòzhě	连	or
11	书	shū	名	book
12	旅游	lǚyóu	动	to travel
13	送	sòng	动	to give
14	实用	shíyòng	形	useful
15	特色	tèsè	名	specialty, hallmark, characteristic
16	有名	yǒumíng	形	famous, well-known
17	轻	qīng	形	light (not heavy)
18	除了……还……	chúle……hái……		outside of…also…
19	工艺品	gōngyìpǐn	名	arts and crafts
20	扇子	shànzi	名	fan
21	中国结	zhōngguójié	名	Chinese knot
22	剪纸	jiǎnzhǐ	名	paper-cutting, paper-cut
23	泥人	nírén	名	clay figurine
24	脸谱	liǎnpǔ	名	facial makeup used in Chinese opera (here, masks based on Chinese opera)
25	爸爸	bàba	名	father
26	画	huàr	名	painting
27	闻名	wénmíng		renowned, famous
28	油画	yóuhuàr	名	oil painting
29	幅	fú	量	[a measure word, for paintings]
30	爷爷	yéye	名	grandfather
31	画	huà	动	to paint
32	……家	……jiā	名	[indicates a specialist or a professional in a field of work]
33	画家	huàjiā	名	painter

专名词 • Proper Names

34	大芬村	dàfēncūn		Dafen village

四、词语解释 · WORD USAGE

(一)、要……了、快……了

"要……了"、"快……了"、"快要……了"与"就要……了"意思差不多,也表示即将发生某件事情或出现某种情况、状态。但用法有所不同,详见"辨析"部分。

The patterns "要…了," "快…了," "快要…了," and "就要……了" all have about the same meaning. They all indicate that a situation or condition will occur in the future. In use, however, they do have some slight differences. (See the Distinguish section below.)

例如: 1. 要下雨了,我们快回房间吧。
2. 马上快要睡觉了,别吃东西了。
3. 快毕业了,我要去找工作。

我们来造句 · Make your own sentence

_____

(二)、除了……还……

"除了……还……"的意思是在原来已经有的情况或数量基础上再加上其它的。也可以说"除了……以外,还……"。"除了……"、"除了……以外"还可以和"都"一起用,组成"除了……都……"、"除了……以外,都……"的形式,表达不包括前面小句中提到的情况或数量,其它的都包括的意思。

The pattern "除了…还…" is used to express an addition to a basic situation or quantity. The patterns "除了…以外, 还…," "除了…," and "除了…以外" have the same meaning. 除了 can also be used with 都 to form the patterns "除了…都" and "除了…以外, 都…," which express inclusion of not just one condition or quantity, but of all such situations or quantities.

例如: 1. 这件事除了他知道,还有我知道。
2. 他除了不吃鱼以外,还不吃虾。
3. 除了星期天以外,他每天都要工作。
4. 除了不喜欢游泳以外,他什么运动都喜欢。

我们来造句 · Make your own sentence

_____

(三)、<u>这样吧</u>,我送你一幅

在这里,"这样吧"的意思是表示自己做了一个决定后向别人提出建议。常在会话中作插入语或出现在第一个小句中,后面的小句则是解释或说明"这样"的具体内容,告诉对方"怎么样"。

Here, 这样吧 indicates a decision on the speaker's part or a suggestion. In conversations, it is usually used as a parenthetical expression or appears in the first of many clauses. The following clauses explain what is meant by 这样, describing the specifics of the speaker's decision or suggestion.

例如： 1. 这样吧，我还有事，你们先走吧，别等我了。

2. 这样吧，我们一起给艾美丽买个生日蛋糕吧。

我们来造句 • Make your own sentence

_____

○ 辨析：Distinguish between the following words

☛ 快……了"、"快要……了"、"就要……了"和"要……了"

"快……了"、"快要……了"、"就要……了"和"要……了"意思差不多，都表示即将发生某件事情或出现某种情况、状态。这组句式中，基本的形式是"要……了"。在"要……了"的基础上加上"快"、"就"，起到了加强"快"、"时间短"的意思。因此，"快要……了"和"就要……了"比"要……了"的语气和程度要重一些。在使用的时候"快要……了"、"快……了"与"就要……了"、"要……了"有所不同。在"快……了"、"快要……了"的句中不可以出现表示具体时间的词，例如：1.星期三（就）要放假了。（√）2.星期三快（要）放假了。（×）另外，"快……了"可以单独成句，其它的则不可以。

例如： 1. A:车什么时候到？B:快了。（√）

2. A:车什么时候到？B:快要了。（×）

3. A:车什么时候到？B:（就）要了。（×）

The patterns "要…了," "快…了," "快要…了," and "就要……了" all have about the same meaning. They all indicate that a situation or condition will occur in the future. In use, however, they do have some slight differences. The most basic pattern among these is "要…了." Adding 快 or 就 to this pattern emphasizes speed or a short time. Because of this, "快要…了" and "就要…了" are much more emphatic than "要…了."

Additionally, "就要…了" and "要…了" may be used with words indicating specific times, so "星期三（就）要放假了" is correct. In contrast, "快要…了" and "快…了" may not be used with words indicating a specific time. "星期三快（要）放假了" is incorrect.

Moreover, only 快了 can be used alone is a sentence, so "A:车什么时候到？B:快了。" is correct. However "A:车什么时候到？B:快要了。" and "A:车什么时候到？B:（就）要了。" are incorrect.

☛ "或者"和"还是"

"或者"和"还是"都有表示选择的意思，但两者不一样，"或者"表示肯定的选择，"还是"表示疑问的选择。"A或者B"的意思是两个都可以，但要选择一个。"A还是B"的意思是两个中只能选择一个。例如：1.我们星期三或者星期四见面都可以。2.你去打篮球还是去游泳？

或者 and 还是 both indicate a choice. However, 或者 is used in affirmative sentences, indicating that two choices are both acceptable. 还是, on the other hand, is used in interrogative sentences, indicating that only one of two options can be chosen.

For example: 1. 我们星期三或者星期四见面都可以。
2. 你去打篮球还是去游泳？

五、汉语知识 • Chinese Knowledge

"动词+的"的意义和用法 • The pattern "verb+的"

汉语中，"动词+的"常常用来修饰限制后面的名词，比如："他开的车"、"我买的书"、"妈妈做的饭"等等。在使用过程中，"的"后面的名词常常可以省略，只用"动词+的"来表示要表达的名词，比如"吃的"意思是"吃的东西"，"穿的"意思是"穿的衣服"。"动词+的"在使用的时候与名词的意义和用法相同。

The pattern "verb+的" is often used to restrict the meanings of nouns, as in 他开的车, 我买的书, and 妈妈做的饭. In another common use the noun following the pattern "verb+的" can often be omitted, with the pattern itself acting as a noun in the sentence. For example, 吃的 can be understood as 吃的东西, and 穿的 can be understood to mean 穿的衣服.

例如：1. A：你觉得谁做的菜最好吃？
B：妈妈做的最好吃。
2. A：这是谁买的剪纸？
B．小王买的。

六、相关链接 • Related Terms: popular Chinese presents for foreigners

受外国朋友欢迎的中国礼物 • Popular Chinese presents for foreigners

1	中国茶	zhōngguóchá	Chinese tea
2	中国工艺品	zhōnguógōngyìpǐn	Chinese arts and crafts
3	中国画	zhōngguóhuàr	Chinese paintings
4	中国书法	zhōngguóshūfǎ	Chinese calligraphy

七、文化生活小贴士 • CULTURAL TIPS: ARTS & TABOOS

（一）、中国画与中国书法 • Chinese painting and Chinese calligraphy

中国画：汉族传统绘画形式是用毛笔蘸水、墨、彩作画于绢或纸上，这种画种被称为"中国画"，简称"国画"。题材可分人物、山水、花鸟等，技法可分工笔和写意等。

A brush dipped in black or colored inks is used for the traditional painting style of the Han ethnicity. This style of painting is called 中国画, or 国画 for short. Subject matter includes people, landscapes, flowers, birds, and other content. Painting styles can be divided into two main categories: 工笔 (realistic painting) and 写意笔 (expressive painting).

中国书法：中国汉字书法，又称"书法"，是人们书写汉字的一种方法。主要分为"软笔书法"和"硬笔书法"，是中国特有的一种传统文化艺术。

Chinese calligraphy, or 书法, refers to various ways of writing Chinese characters. Calligraphy can broadly be divided into two categories: 软笔, or brush calligraphy, and 硬笔, or pen and ink calligraphy. It is one of China's unique, traditional art forms.

（二）、中国人送礼的禁忌 • Taboo presents in China

在中国，特别是广东，很多人不喜欢"4"，因为"4"的发音听起来像是"死"，是不吉利的。送礼物时一般不送"4"这个数量的东西。再如，白色虽有纯洁无瑕之意，但中国人在一些场合中认为白色与黑色一样，都表示哀丧、灾凶。中国喜欢红色，认为红色是喜庆、祥和、欢庆的象征，所以受到人们的普遍喜爱。另外，中国人认为不能送给老人钟表，因"送钟"与"送终"的发音一样。给夫妻或情人不能送梨，因为 "梨"与"离"谐音。还有，不能给健康人送药品，不能为异性朋友送贴身的用品等。

In much of China, and especially in Guangdong, many people dislike the number 四, because it is pronounced similarly to 死 (die) and is, therefore, considered unlucky. When giving presents to Chinese people, it is best to avoid giving four of anything. Similarly, it is best to avoid giving a clock to the elderly, since 送种 is pronounced similarly to 送终 (arrange funerals for senior family members), and to avoid giving pears to married or dating couples, since 梨 is pronounced similarly to 离 (to part or separate).

Additionally, colors have special significance in Chinese culture. While the color white can represent purity, in many circumstances, Chinese people believe it represents death or disaster, much like the color black. White presents should be avoided in many circumstances. In contrast, the color red in Chinese culture represents joy, good fortune, and festivity in most circumstances.

Finally, Chinese people do not give intimate items (such as undergarments or lingerie) to friends who are members of the opposite sex.

八、练习 • Exercises

（一）、填上合适的词语 • Fill in the blanks with appropriate words

看望_____、_____　　爱好_____、_____

实用的_____　　有名的_____　　普通的_____

（二）、选词填空 • Fill in the blanks with the words provided

▶ 实用　普通　爱好　放假　看望　有名　未来　特色

1. 这种植物太_____了，到处都是。
2. 明天学校_____，我们一起去看电影吧。
3. 这些杯子漂亮是漂亮就是不太_____。
4. 我从来没有见过这样的鱼，它很有_____。
5. 他最大的_____就是旅游。
6. 那家饭馆很_____，每天都有很多人去那里吃饭。
7. 他经常回学校_____老师。
8. 我相信你的_____会越来越好！

▶ 或者　还是

1. 去医院看病人可以买花_____买水果。
2. 你星期一有空儿_____星期三有空儿？
3. 你喜欢中国结_____喜欢剪纸？
4. 去哈尔滨旅游最好冬天去，_____夏天去。

（三）、用所给的词语完成句子

Fill in the blanks with sentences using the words given in parentheses

1. A：你觉得冬天去哪儿旅游比较合适？
   B：_____。（或者）
2. A：你一般怎么过生日？
   B：_____。（除了……还）
3. A：你最近在忙什么？
   B：_____。（快要……了）
4. A：你为什么喜欢她？
   B：_____。（既……又）
5. A：你怎么买了这么多工艺品？
   B：_____。（要……了）

（四）、填量词 • Fill in the blanks with the words provided

个　幅　把　杯　份

一_____钱包　　　一_____礼物
一_____茶　　　　一_____扇子
一_____画

（五）、解释下面句中"看"的意思和用法

Explain the meaning of 看 in the following sentences

1. 平时我喜欢一个人在家**看**书或者看电视。
2. 你**看**我穿这条裙子怎么样？
3. 我也是第一次碰到这样的事，没有经验，只能试试**看**。
4. 去医院**看**病人可以买些花或者水果。

（六）、用"还是"与"或者"和你的朋友讨论周末出游的事

Use 还是 and 或者 to have a discussion about where to go this weekend

（七）、根据课文提到的一些礼品的描述，用抢答的形式猜猜它是什么

Based on the sentences given below, guess what presents are being described. All of them appear in this lesson.

1. 它是夏天用的，能产生风，让你感觉很凉快。
2. 它是可以喝的，需要用热水泡，泡完后你会看到很多叶子，闻起来很香。
3. 它是一种工艺品，上面有各种好看的图案，它可以贴在墙上，它是用纸做的，用剪刀剪的。
4. 它是一种工艺品，它不大，很可爱，它是用泥做的，它像一个小孩子。
5. 它是中国特有的一种艺术，它写在一张纸上，是黑白色的，它是用毛笔写的，写的是汉字。
6. 它用的是毛笔，墨水，有黑白的，也有彩色的，在一张纸上画的，经常画山水、花鸟。

（八）、课堂活动 • Classroom Activity

1. 新年快来了，你要去买新年礼物。下面是一张超市购物的清单，请模仿这份清单写一份新的清单，和你的同学分享。说说你买的礼物中，要送给谁什么礼物，为什么？

New Year's is coming soon. You want to buy some New Year's presents. Below is a shopping list. Imitate the list to write your own shopping list. Tell your classmates what you will buy, for whom, and why.

2010.12.23 12:30			
收银机：06 收银员：0971			
货号/品名/单位	单价	数量	小计
00112 玩具熊/个	100	1	100
10234 巧克力/盒	70	1	70
01987 棉拖鞋/双	30	1	30
05553 外套/件	220	1	220
08932 圣袜/只	15	3	45
10843 杯子/个	25	1	25
09821 包/个	30	1	30
数量：9 合计：520.00			
付款：人民币现金550.00			
找零：人民币现金30.00			
谢谢惠顾！欢迎下次光临！			

2. 提前准备一份神秘礼物，在上面的课堂活动结束后抽签和全班同学互换礼物。

   Prepare a present for the class and keep it hidden. The whole class will draw lots to see with whom to exchange presents.

（九）、来聊天儿吧 • Discuss

1. 假如你下个星期就要回国了，谈谈你想带什么礼物给你的朋友。

   If you were going back to your home country next week, what presents would you take back for friends?

2. 你最好的朋友要结婚了，谈谈你要送什么礼物给他。

   If your best friend were planning to get married, what present would you give him or her?

3. 假设你准备来中国学汉语，你会带什么礼物给你的中国朋友，用几句话介绍一下你的礼物。

   If you were coming back to China from your home country, what presents would you bring for Chinese friends? Try to use several sentences to explain.

第十五课 / LESSON 15

中国值得去的地方太多了
PLACES WORTH VISITING IN CHINA ARE TOO MANY TO LIST

这一课我们将学到 • In this lesson we will study the following:
1. 与在中国旅游有关的内容
2. 重点词语：你有什么可介绍的……、特别是
3. 汉语知识：语音、韵律在汉语中的重要性

一、课文 • Text

（艾美丽在给吴帅打电话 • Emily is giving Wu Shuai a telephone call）

 吴帅： 喂？
Hi?

 艾美丽： 吴帅，我是艾美丽。我打算下星期去旅游，你有什么可介绍的吗？
Wu Shuai, I am Emily. Next week I plan to go traveling. What places can you tell me about?

 吴帅： 中国值得去的地方太多了。有很多俗语都是介绍中国旅游胜地的。像"上有天堂，下有苏杭"，说的是苏州和杭州；"桂林山水甲天下"，说的是桂林；"五岳归来不看山，黄山归来不看岳"，说的是黄山。
Places worth visiting in China are too many to list. We have many common sayings, all of which describe China's famous scenic spots. For example, "Above is Heaven; below, SuHang," which is talking about Suzhou and Hangzhou. "Guilin's landscape is first in the world" talks about Guilin. "After coming back from the Five Mountains, you won't want to see others. After coming back from Yellow Mountain, you won't want to see another" talks about HuangShan.

 艾美丽： 我只有……我只有五天的时间，你看怎么安排好啊？
I just have…I just have five days. How do you think I can plan my time best?

吴帅： 你最想去看什么？自然风光？名胜古迹？还是风土人情？
What do you most want to see? Natural scenery? Scenic and historic sites? Regional cultures?

 艾美丽： 我最想看（是）名胜古迹，特别是古老的园林、宫殿和陵墓。
I most want to see scenic and historic sites, especially old parks, palaces or tombs.

 吴帅： 那我推荐你去西安和北京吧。
Then, I'd recommend you go to Xi'an and Beijing.

 艾美丽： 西安？就是发现兵马俑的地方吗？
Xi'an? That's where they discovered the terracotta warriors, right?

 吴帅： 对。那里不仅有兵马俑，还有你感兴趣的园林和宫殿。另外还有宝塔和寺庙，它们都有许多古老的故事和传说。
Right. There, not only do they have the terracotta warriors, but they also have many parks and palaces of the sort you're interested in. Outside of those, they also have pagodas and temples. They all have many old tales and legends told about them.

 艾美丽： 嗯，那太好了！那就去西安吧！
Umm, then great! Then I'll go to Xi'an.

 吴帅： 其实我也一直很想去，我和你一块儿去吧！
Actually, I've always wanted to go. How about you and I going together?

 艾美丽： 好啊，你喜欢跟团去还是自助游？
OK. Do you like traveling with a tour group or on your own?

 吴帅： 我想自助游，因为这样我们可以在自己喜欢的地方呆久点儿。
I'd want to travel on our own, because that way we can stay a bit longer in any places we like.

 艾美丽： 好的，那我们今晚订机票和酒店吧。
Ok, then can we book tickets and a hotel tonight?

 吴帅： 没问题，晚上再联系。
No problem. Tonight, let's talk again.

 艾美丽： 嗯，好，再见。
Umm, OK, see you later.

 吴帅： 再见。
See you later.

二、根据课文回答问题 • ANSWER THE FOLLOWING QUESTIONS ACCORDING TO THE TEXT

1. 如果想看名胜古迹去哪儿比较好？

   _____

2. 西安最有名的旅游景点是什么？

   _____

3. 吴帅喜欢跟团游还是自助游？为什么？

   _____

4. 课文中都提到了哪些中国有名的旅游城市？

   _____

三、生词 • VOCABULARY

1	值得	zhídé	动	to be worth, deserve
2	俗语	súyǔ	名	common saying, axiom
3	胜地	shèngdì	名	famous scenic spots
4	天堂	tiāntáng	名	Heaven, Paradise
5	山	shān	名	mountain
6	（江、河、湖、海）水	shuǐ	名	water(as in rivers, streams, lakes and seas)
7	山水	shānshuǐ	名	landscape
8	甲	jiǎ	名	first, best
9	天下	tiānxià	名	world
10	岳	yuè	名	a tall mountain
11	安排	ānpái	动、名	to plan; a plan
12	自然	zìrán	名	natural
13	风光	fēngguāng	名	scenery, view, sight
14	古迹	gǔjì	名	historic sites
15	风土	fēngtǔ	名	local conditions, regional customs
16	人情	rénqíng	名	customs, culture
17	古老	gǔlǎo	形	old, ancient
18	园林	yuánlín	名	park, garden
19	宫殿	gōngdiàn	名	palace
20	陵墓	língmù	名	tomb, mausoleum
21	发现	fāxiàn	动、名	to discover; a discovery
22	兵马俑	bīngmǎyǒng	名	the terracotta warriors

23	塔	tǎ	名	pagoda, tower
24	宝塔	bǎotǎ	名	(formal for) pagoda
25	寺庙	sìmiào	名	temple
26	许多	xǔduō	副	many, much
27	故事	gùshì	名	story
28	传说	chuánshuō	名	folk tale, legend
29	一直	yìzhí	副	for a long time, always
30	团	tuán	名	travel in a tour group
31	自助	zìzhù		help oneself
32	自助游	zìzhùyóu		plan one's own vacation
33	呆	dāi	动	to stay
34	机票	jīpiào	名	airplane ticket
35	酒店	jiǔdiàn	名	hotel

专名词 • Proper Names

36	苏州	sūzhōu		Suzhou
37	杭州	hángzhōu		Hangzhou
38	桂林	guìlín		Guilin
39	黄山	huángshān		Huang Mountain
40	西安	xī'ān		Xi'an

四、词语解释 • Word Usage

（一）、你有什么**可**介绍的吗？

在这里，"可"是"可以"、"值得"、"有必要"的意思，后面常跟"动词+的"，组成名词性短语。"有什么可……的"常表示疑问或反问的语气。否定形式"没什么可……的"则常用于肯定的语气。"可"还和一些单音节动词组成形容词，比如"可笑"、"可恨"、"可爱"、"可怜"等等。

Here, 可 means "can," "to be worthwhile," or "ought to." Followed by a verb and 的, it forms a word that functions as a noun. The pattern "有什么可…的" can indicate a literal or rhetorical question. The negative response would be "没什么可…的," which is emphatic. 可 can also be combined with a single-character verb to form an adjective similar to those ending in "–able" in English, such as, 可笑, 可恨, 可爱, 可怜.

例如： 1. 中国有很多可去的地方。

2. 你还有什么可解释的吗？

3. 这有什么可说的？（反问句，意思是没什么值得说的）

4. 对这件事我没什么可说的。

5. 等人的时候没什么好做的，只好玩手机。

我们来造句 • Make your own sentence

___

（二）、**特别是**古老的园林、宫殿和陵墓

在这里，"特别是"的意思是表示在所说的或发生的事情中最突出、最重要的意思。通常放在后面的小句中。

Here, 特别是 indicates the most exceptional or important part of a discussion or event. It is most often used in the second of two clauses.

   例如：1. 我最喜欢吃中国菜，特别是四川菜。
      2. 一个人在国外生活很不容易，特别是生病的时候。

我们来造句 • Make your own sentence

___

○ 课文注释：Key Points in the Text

☛ 上有天堂，下有苏杭

"上有天堂，下有苏杭"是人们赞美苏州和杭州的一句俗语，意思是：天上最美的地方是天堂，地上（人间）最美的地方是苏州和杭州。

This is a common saying used in praise of Suzhou and Hangzhou. It can be understood as "Outside of Earth, the most beautiful place is Heaven. On Earth, the most beautiful places are Suzhou and Hangzhou."

☛ 桂林山水甲天下

"桂林山水甲天下"是人们赞美桂林山水的一句俗语，意思是：桂林山水是天下第一美丽的地方。"甲"在这里是"第一"、"最好"的意思。

This is a common phrase used in praise of Guilin. It means that Guilin's sights are the world's most beautiful. Here, 甲 has the same meaning as 第一 or 最好.

☛ 五岳归来不看山，黄山归来不看岳

"五岳归来不看山，黄山归来不看岳"是赞美黄山的名句，中国人把著名的五座山（"泰山、华山、嵩山、衡山、恒山"）称作"五岳"。"五岳归来不看山"的意思是：看完五座著名的山，回来后就不想再看别的山了，如果看了黄山，回来后就不想看"五岳"了。意思是黄山是最美的山。

This is a common phrase used in praise of Huangshan and the Five Holy Mountains (泰山、华山、嵩山、衡山、and 恒山). It means that the Five Holy Mountains and Huangshan are so beautiful that after visiting them, a traveler would be content without ever seeing another mountain.

五、汉语知识 • Chinese Knowledge

语音、韵律在汉语中的重要性 • The importance of meter and sound

因为汉字是"音、形、义"一体化的,所以人们在选择语言材料进行表达时也会考虑语音的因素,也就是说,语音在汉语组词造句的规律中占有重要地位。比如:我们国家(√) 我国家(×) 我国(√) 我们国(×)

Since Chinese characters contain meaning and sound in a single form that occupies a single square, preferences for balance in speaking and writing developed based on numbers of characters. For example, both 我国 and 我们国家 are correct, because a single-character pronoun is followed by a single-character noun, while a two-character pronoun is followed by a two-character noun. Meanwhile, 我国家 and 我们国 are incorrect, because they do not maintain the same balance.

六、相关链接 • Related Terms: China's famous scenic and historical sites

中国著名的名胜古迹 • China's famous scenic and historical sites

1	西安	xī'ān	Xi'an
	秦始皇陵	qínshǐhuánglíng	Mausoleum of the first Qin emperor
	大雁塔	dàyàntǎ	Wild Goose Pagoda
	碑林	bēilín	The Forest of Steles
2	北京	běijīng	Peking
	故宫	gùgōng	The Forbidden City
	颐和园	yíhéyuán	The Summer Palace
	明十三陵	míngshísānlíng	The Ming tombs
3	苏州	sūzhōu	Suzhou
	拙政园	zhuōzhèngyuán	The Administrator's Garden
	沧浪亭	cānglàngtíng	Surging Wave Pavilion
	狮子林	shīzilín	Lion Grove
	留园	liúyuán	The Lingering Garden
4	敦煌	dūnhuáng	Dunhuang
	莫高窟	mògāokū	The Mogao Grottoes
5	桂林	guìlín	Guilin
	漓江	líjiāng	The Li River
6	湖南	húnán	Hunan

	洞庭湖	dòngtínghú	Dongting Lake
7	江西	jiāngxī	Jiangxi
	鄱阳湖	póyánghú	Poyang Lake
	庐山	lúshān	Lu Mountain
8	江苏	jiāngsū	Jiangsu
	太湖	tàihú	Tai lake
9	杭州	hángzhōu	Hangzhou
	西湖	xīhú	Xi Lake
10	安徽	ānhūi	Anhui
	黄山	huángshān	Huang Mountain
11	山东	shāndōng	Shandong
	泰山	tàishān	Tai Mountain
12	四川	sìchūan	Sichuan
	三峡	sānxiá	The Three Gorges
	九寨沟	jiǔzhàigōu	Jiuzhaigou
13	云南	yúnnán	Yunnan
	昆明	kūnmíng	Kunming
	大理	dàlǐ	Dali
	香格里拉	xiānggélǐlā	Shangrila
14	内蒙古	nèiménggǔ	Inner Mongolia
	呼伦贝尔大草原	hūlúnbèiěrdàcǎoyuán	The Hulun Buir Grassland

七、文化生活小贴士 • Cultural Tips: travel websites

订特价机票和酒店的网站

Good websites for booking discount flights and hotels are quna.com and ctrip.com.

八、练习 • Exercises

（一）、填上合适的词语 • Fill in the blanks with appropriate words

值得_____、_____　　　安排_____、_____

许多_____、_____　　　自助_____、_____

风土_____　　名胜_____　　自然_____

（二）、选词填空 • Fill in the blanks with the words provided

值得　　俗语　　古老　　发现　　许多　　联系　　一直　　安排

1. 苏州有很多_____的园林。
2. 考完试以后他才_____很多题都写错了。
3. 学汉语虽然要用很多时间，但是_____。
4. 他经常上网和家人_____。
5. 我们今天学了_____有意思的俗语。
6. 我没有旅游的经验，就听你的_____吧。
7. 毕业后他就_____在找工作，但到现在也没找到。
8. "桂林山水甲天下"是很有名的_____。

（三）、用所给词语完成句子

Fill in the blanks with sentences using the words given in parentheses

1. A：最近怎么没看见小张？
   B：_____。（一直）
2. A：放假时我们去哪儿旅游？
   B：_____。（安排）
3. A：这个地方太难找了！
   B：_____。（值得）
4. A：你有张经理的电话吗？
   B：_____。（联系）
5. A：星期天你去哪儿玩了？
   B：_____。（呆）

（四）、解释下列俗语 • Explain these common sayings in your own words

1. "上有天堂，下有苏杭"
2. "桂林山水甲天下"
3. "五岳归来不看山，黄山归来不看岳"

（五）、在老师的帮助下把下列景点进行归类

With your teacher's help, place the following locations into appropriate categories

秦始皇陵　　西湖　　黄山　　明十三陵　　拙政园
狮子林　　　留园　　漓江　　庐山　　　　太湖
泰山　　　　三峡　　九寨沟　沧浪亭

陵墓

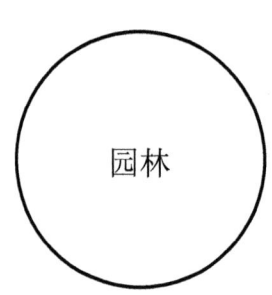
园林

自然风光

（六）、用"可"、"特别是"改写句子 • Rewrite the sentences using the words provided

▶ 可

1. 深圳有很多值得去的地方。
2. 商店有很多我需要买的东西。
3. 我觉得跟他没什么话说。
4. 他有很多值得学习的地方。

▶ 特别是

1. 深圳很热，夏天最热。
2. 我喜欢运动，最喜欢打网球。
3. 他喜欢看书，最喜欢看旅游方面的书。
4. 我觉得汉语很难，汉字最难。

（七）、成段表达 • Prepare a short speech for class

1. 介绍自己国家的名胜古迹、自然风光，或者风土人情并推荐一个好地方。

Introduce your own country's scenic or historical sites, natural landscapes, or local customs. Recommend a travel destination.

2. 描述一个你喜欢的城市。

Describe a city that you like.

3. 用下面的词语向你的朋友介绍一个中国旅游的好地方。

Use the following words to recommend a Chinese travel destination to a friend

俗语　　　许多　　　古老　　　旅游　　　胜地
不仅……而且　　一直　　　另外　　　值得

（八）、在一张中国地图上找出课文及相关链接中提到的旅游景点

Find the places of interest mentioned in the Related Terms on the map below.

（九）、来聊天吧 • Discuss

1. 你去过中国哪些地方？讲一个有关旅游的有意思的故事。

Where have you been in China? Tell a story about an interesting experience you had while traveling.

2. 你喜欢去哪儿旅游？为什么？

Where do you enjoy traveling? Why?

第十六课 / LESSON 16

祝你一路顺风!
MAY FAVORABLE WINDS SPEED YOU ON YOUR WAY!

这一课我们将学到 • In this lesson we will study the following:
1. 与送别有关的内容
2. 重点词语：不管……都…… 、还……吗
3. 汉语知识：汉语中的古汉语

一、课文 • TEXT

（在深圳大学的一个餐厅门口 • In front of one of Shenzhen University's cafeterias）

 艾美丽： 时间过得真快呀，我已经在深圳呆了四年了。
Time has passed really quickly. I have already stayed four years in China.

 艾美丽的同学： 是啊，我还记得我们第一次见面的时候的情景，现在已经到送你回国的时候了。
You have. I still remember the circumstances in which we first met. Now, we've already arrived at the time for you to go back to your country.

 艾美丽： （对送行的人说） 有一些话一直没有机会说，现在可以说了。很感谢你们这四年来的照顾，我在中国过得很开心，现在要走了，我很舍不得你们，也舍不得这里的生活。
(To the people sending her off) I have a few things that all along I haven't had opportunity to say. Now I can say them. Thank you very much for these four years' caring for me. I've spent my time in China very happily, and now I have to go. I'm very unwilling to part from you and very unwilling to part from my life here.

 艾美丽的同学： 我们也一样，很高兴能跟你一起过这四年，我们也很舍不得你。中国有句古话："海内存知己，天涯若比邻。"今后不管在哪里，我们都会想念你的。
We also feel the same. We're very happy we could spend these four years with you. We're also very unwilling to part with you. China has one old saying: "As long as there is a friend in this world who knows your heart, even though separated by a great distance, it is as though you are close."

艾美丽: 我会好好珍惜这一段时光的，也希望你们以后能过得开心。
I will really treasure this time. I also hope you all live happily in the future.

艾美丽的同学: 以后有机会就回来看看我们，希望你那时候别忘了我们。
In the future, if you have an opportunity, come back and see us. I hope when that time comes you won't forget us.

艾美丽的同学: 我不担心，我们有人质呢，有吴帅在，还害怕她不回来吗？
I am not worried. We have a hostage. We have Wu Shuai here. How can you still fear that she won't come back?

艾美丽: 怎么会呢？我一定会回来的，到时候我们再聚。好。你们多保重。
How could it be? I certainly will come back. When that time arrives, we'll get together again. OK. You all take good care of yourselves.

艾美丽的同学: 嗯，你也一样，保持联系。祝你一路顺风！
Umm, you also do the same. Keep in contact. May favorable winds speed you on your journey.

艾美丽: 好，谢谢你们！再见了！
OK. Thank you all. See you again.

同学们: 再见！
See you again.

在深圳宝安机场候机室 • In a waiting room in the Bao'an airport

艾美丽: 快要登机了，我要走了。
Soon, I need to board the plane. I need to go.

吴帅: 你一个人路上要小心，到了以后马上打个电话。
You be careful on the way. After you arrive, immediately make a telephone call.

艾美丽: 好，放心吧。你也要照顾好自己。
OK. Relax, OK? You also should take good care of yourself.

吴帅: 我会的。替我问候你的家人！
I will. On my behalf, say hello to your family.

艾美丽: 好，谢谢！
OK. Thanks.

吴帅: 一路平安！再见！
May your journey be peaceful. See you again.

艾美丽: 再见！
See you again.

二、根据课文回答问题 • Answer the following questions according to the text

1. 艾美丽在深圳呆了几年了？

2. 艾美丽跟同学们说了些什么话？

3. "海内存知己，天涯若比邻。"这句话是什么意思？

4. 艾美丽的同学为什么不担心艾美丽不回来？

三、生词 • Vocabulary

1	一路	yílù		journey, trip
2	顺风	shùnfēng		tail wind, favorable wind
3	一路顺风	yílùshùnfēng		[a wish for a pleasant trip]
4	情景	qíngjǐng	名	situation, circumstance
5	送行	sòngxíng	动	to see someone off, to send someone off
6	照顾	zhàogù	动	to care for, to take care of
7	舍不得	shěbude		reluctant to part with
8	生活	shēnghuó	名、动	life, lifestyle; to live
9	句	jù	量	[a measure word, for a sentence]
10	古	gǔ	形	old, classical, ancient
11	海	hǎi	名	sea, ocean
12	存	cún	动	to be, to exist
13	知己	zhījǐ	名	intimate friend, close friend
14	天涯	tiānyá	名	the remotest corner of the earth
15	若	ruò	动	to seem as though
16	比邻	bǐlín		neighbors, close neighbors
17	今后	jīnhòu	名	from now on, after today
18	不管……都……	bùguǎn……dōu……		[see Word Usage]
19	想念	xiǎngniàn	动	to miss
20	珍惜	zhēnxī	动	to treasure, to cherish
21	段	duàn	量	[a measure word, here, for a time]

22	时光	shíguāng	名	time, period
23	人质	rénzhì	名	hostage
24	害怕	hàipà	动	to fear, to be afraid
25	保重	bǎozhòng	动	to take care of oneself
26	保持	bǎochí	动	to keep up, to maintain a status
27	候机室	hòujīshì		airport lounge, waiting room
28	登	dēng	动	to ascend, to board
29	登机	dēngjī		to board a plane
30	小心	xiǎoxīn	动、形	to be careful, careful
31	放心	fàngxīn	动	to relax
32	替	tì	动	to take the place of, to replace
33	问候	wènhòu	动	to greet, to say hello
34	平安	píng'ān	形	safe, untroubled
35	一路平安	yílùpíngān		[a wish for a safe trip]

四、词语解释 • Word Usage

（一）、不管……都……

"不管……都……"的意思表示在任何条件下结果或结论都是一样的。书面语中常用"无论……都……"来表达。"不管"的后面通常有"肯定+否定"的动词或形容词，也可以是疑问词，用来表示"任何"的意思。"不管……都……"

The pattern "不管…都…" indicates that an outcome is the same under any conditions. "无论…都…" expresses the same meaning in the written language. 不管 is followed by an affirmative verb or adjective, then a negative verb or adjective. It can also be followed by a question word, by which "anyone," "anything," "any situation," etc., is suggested.

例如： 1. 不管天气好不好，我们都要去上课。
2. 不管你去不去，我都会去。
3. 不管我说什么，他都不听。
4. 不管怎么样，你都应该帮助他。
5. 不管是谁，我都不告诉。

我们来造句 • Make your own sentence

___

（二）、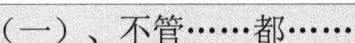

在这里，"还……吗"表达反问的语气，"还害怕她不回来吗？"的意思是："不怕她不回来"。也可以与"难道"一起连用。

Here the pattern "还…吗"emphasizes a rhetorical question. "还害怕她不回来吗？" has the same meaning as "不怕她不会来." This pattern can also be used together with 难道 (3).

例如：1. 她还不漂亮吗？（意思是：她漂亮）

2. 你觉得他还会原谅你吗？（意思是：他不会原谅你）

3. 难道我还不知道这件事很重要吗？（意思是：我知道这件事很重要）

我们来造句 • Make your own sentence

_____

课文注释：Key Points in the Text

"海内存知己，天涯若比邻。"出自唐代著名诗人王勃的一首送别诗。
The sentence "海内存知己，天涯若比邻" is from a poem by Wang Bo, a famous Tang dynasty poet.

全诗是这样的：　　　　城阙辅三秦，风烟望五津。

与君离别意，同是宦游人。

海内存知己，天涯若比邻。

无为在歧路，儿女共沾巾。

这首诗的大意是：（即将告别）由三秦环绕着的都城长安，（透过迷漫的）风烟（似乎能）望见（巴蜀的）五大渡口。（我）同您（此时）都怀有惜别的心情，（因为我们）都是离乡在外做官的人。（只要）四海之内有着知心朋友，（即使）远隔万里（也）如近在咫（zhǐ）尺。不要因为（我们要）在岔路口（分别），（就像）男女青年（一样），一起（流泪而）沾湿手巾。其中"海内存知己，天涯若比邻。"最有名。

The poem's basic content involves the poet's saying good-bye to a close friend. "Changan is surrounded by the country of Qin's three divisions. Through a veil of smoke and mist, it seems the five crossing points into Sichuan can hazily be seen. You and I both feel a strong reluctance to part. We are both leaving our hometown to assume positions as officials. <u>As long as there is a friend in this world who knows your heart, even though separated by a great distance, it is as though you are close.</u> As we arrive at a fork in our commonly traveled road, let us not be like sentimental youths; let us not soak our handkerchiefs with tears." "海内存知己，天涯若比邻" is the best-known of the sentences from this poem.

五、汉语知识 • Chinese Knowledge

汉语中的古代汉语 • Classical, or ancient, Chinese

相对于现代汉语而言，中国古代时人们使用的语言，叫古代汉语。现代汉语是在古代汉语基础上发展来的，因此现代汉语中还保留了很多古代汉语的词汇和语法，因此适当了解一些古代汉语的知识对学习现代汉语是很有好处的。

As opposed to the language spoken and written in modern times, what is called 古代汉语 is the written language studied and used prior to the mid-1800s. Modern Chinese developed upon the foundation of classical Chinese. Because of this, many classical words and sayings have been retained in modern Chinese. Therefore, becoming familiar with certain classical sayings is advantageous even when learning the modern language.

六、相关链接，汉语中的祝词 • Related Terms: congratulations

1	祝你生日快乐！	zhùnǐ shēngrì kuàilè	Happy birthday
2	祝你中秋节快乐！	zhùnǐ zhōngqiūjié kuàilè	Happy Mid-Autumn Festival
3	祝你圣诞节快乐！	zhùnǐ shèngdànjié kuàilè	Merry Christmas
4	祝你们白头偕老！早生贵子！	zhùnǐmen báitóuxiélǎo! zǎoshēngguìzǐ	May you grow old together and have a child soon
5	祝你心想事成！	zhùnǐ xīnxiǎngshìchéng	May all your dreams come true
6	祝你好运！	zhùnǐ hǎoyùn	Good luck
7	恭喜发财！	gōngxǐ fācái	May you prosper

七、文化生活小贴士，中国的主要节日 • Cultural Tips: major festivals in China

▶ 公历节日：Festivals of the Gregorian calendar

1月1日：元旦	yuándàn	New Year's Day
4月5日：清明节	qīngmíngjié	Tomb-Sweeping Day, Qingming Festival
5月1日：国际劳动节	guójì láodòngjié	May Day, Labour Day
6月1日：国际儿童节	guójì értóngjié	International Children's Day
10月1日：国庆节	guóqìngjié	China's National Day

▶ 农历节日：Festivals of the traditional Chinese calendar

正月（一月）初一：春节	chūnjié	Chinese New Year's Day
正月（一月）十五：元宵节	yuánxiāojié	The Lantern Festival
五月初五：端午节	duānwǔjié	Dragon Boat Festival
八月十五：中秋节	zhōngqiūjié	Mid-Autumn Holiday
九月初九：重阳节	chóngyángjié	The Double Ninth Festival

八、练习 • Exercises

（一）、填上合适的词语 • Fill in the blanks with appropriate words

照顾_____、_____　　　想念_____、_____

珍惜_____、_____　　　保持_____、_____

（二）、选词填空 • Fill in the blanks with the words provided

保重　机会　照顾　想念　珍惜　保持　害怕　情景

1. 很感谢这几年大家对我的_____。
2. 毕业后我们一直_____联系。

3. 我们都很_____在一起学习的日子。

4. 你自己一个人在国外，你要_____身体。

5. 回国一年了，我常常想起跟大家一起玩的时候的_____。

6. 天黑了，我一个人出门有点儿_____。

7. 我已经两年没见我爷爷了，我非常_____他。

8. 我希望有_____去中国旅游。

（三）、用所给词语完成句子

Fill in the blanks with sentences using the words given in parentheses

1. A：我明天就要回国了。
   B：_____。（问候）

2. A：把这只猫送给我好吗？
   B：_____。（舍不得）

3. A：在中国的这段时间你觉得怎么样？
   B：_____。（珍惜）

4. A：你有王老师的电话号码？
   B：_____。（保持）

5. A：再见了，一路平安！
   B：_____。（保重）

6. A：最近一直没见你，忙什么呢？
   B：_____。（照顾）

7. A：今天怎么是王老师给你们上课？
   B：_____。（替）

8. A：你怎么了？看上去不太高兴。
   B：_____。（想念）

（四）、用所学词语表达 • Form sentences using the sentence patterns and words provided

▶ 不管……都

1. 天气好坏都去旅游。　　_____
2. 汉语很难，但还要学。　　_____
3. 同学去不去动物园你都去。　　_____
4. 什么菜都喜欢。　　_____

▶ 还……吗

1. 同学们知道这件事，不用告诉了。　　_____
2. 时间很多，不担心完不成工作。　　_____
3. 菜已经很多了，不用买了。　　_____

4. 大家都明白了，不需要再讲了。 _____

▶ 到时候

1. 你去我家的时候我去接你。 _____
2. 去KTV时，我们一起唱歌。 _____
3. 你想学汉语可以跟我学。 _____
4. 你过生日时我请你吃饭。 _____

▶ 怎么会

1. 他一定会来。 _____
2. 他一定喜欢你送的礼物。 _____
3. 他真的不知道这件事。 _____
4. 这个字学过，应该会写。 _____

（五）、词语连线 • Match words to form short phrases

保持   照顾   保重   想念   珍惜

身体   孩子   家人   联系   友谊

（六）、填量词 • Fill in the blanks with the words provided

首   段   份   家

一_____时光   一_____古诗

一_____工作   一_____公司

（七）、角色扮演：模仿课文内容表演送别的情景

Performance: Imitate the text to simulate seeing someone off.

（八）、你知道中国有关送别的歌吗？

介绍一下你们国家跟送别有关的歌，唱一首给大家听。

Do you know some Chinese songs about sending someone off or saying good-bye?

Tell us about similar songs from your home country and sing for the class.

（九）、来聊天吧 • Discuss

1. 说说你和家人分别时的情景和心情。

   Tell about how you felt or what the situation was the last time you parted from your family.

2. 你就要离开深圳回国了，说说你现在的感觉。

   If you are preparing to leave Shenzhen and return to your home country, how do you feel about it?

参考答案
ANSWERS TO EXERCISES

第一课：明天深圳天气怎么样？

❏ 根据课文回答问题：1.大部分地方都很热 ◆ 2.深圳的冬天不下雪 ◆ 3.台风在中国南方刮 ◆ 4.春天和秋天不冷也不热，挺舒服的。不过，春天比较潮湿，秋天有点儿干燥 ◆ 5.别忘了擦防晒霜，还要带上雨伞

❏ （一）、谈论天气、工作 ◆ 从不下雪、运动 ◆ 天气预报、很好 ◆ 部分地区、同学 ◆ 刮风下雨 ◆ 东南西北 ◆ 上下左右 ◆ 春夏秋冬

❏ （二）、1.零下 ◆ 2.谈论 ◆ 3.从不 ◆ 4.舒服 ◆ 5.气候 ◆ 6.野餐 ◆ 7.干燥 ◆ 8.地区

❏ （三）、1.我从不一个人喝酒 ◆ 2.深圳夏天的天气很热，而且常常下雨 ◆ 3.我能听懂一部分 ◆ 4.我常常给妈妈打电话 ◆ 5.我越来越习惯吃中国菜了 ◆ 6.我看今天会下雨

❏ （四）、1.从低处往高处的意思 ◆ 2.从低处往高处的意思 ◆ 3.把食物拿来的意思 ◆ 4.在动词后面表示动作的结果 ◆ 5.指在什么东西的里面，或指某东西的内容或范围。例如：报纸上、电视上等 ◆ 6.某些东西的上面或里面 ◆ 7.是指做某事，有"进行"、"做"的意思 ◆ 8.没有实在意思，与"早"一起组成"早晨"的意思

❏ （五）、大——小 对——错 ◆ 买——卖 ◆ 上——下 ◆ 肥——瘦 ◆ 冷——热 ◆ 高——矮/低 ◆ 潮湿——干燥 ◆ 多——少 ◆ 快——慢 ◆ 阴——晴 ◆ 左——右 ◆ 开——关 ◆ 前——后 ◆ 黑——白

❏ （六）、1.小王比小张高。小张比小王矮 ◆ 2.坐出租车比坐公交车快。坐公交车比坐出租车慢 ◆ 3.我比他会写的汉字多。他比我会写的汉字少 ◆ 4.啤酒比饮料贵。饮料比啤酒便宜 ◆ 5.从学校到我家比银行到我家远。从银行到我家比学校到我家近 ◆ 6.老师比学生（年龄）大。学生比老师（年龄）小

❏ （七）、香港3月28日晴间多云，最高气温22摄氏度，最低气温14摄氏度 ◆ 东京3月28日 晴，最高气温12摄氏度，最低气温4摄氏度 ◆ 马尼拉3月28日 多云有阵雨，最高气温31摄氏度，最低气温25摄氏度 ◆ 莫斯科3月28日多云转阴，最高气温3摄氏度，最低气温零下7摄氏度

❏ （八）、晴 多云 阴 晴转小雨 阴有中雷阵雨 ◆ 阴有小雨 阴有大雨 阴有暴雨

❏ （九）、11月21日中午到傍晚，多云，有短时牛奶雨，记得带杯子来接牛奶；咖啡风2-3级；沿海的咖啡风风力4级，阵风7级；请戴好口罩。今天最高气温20℃，最低气温15℃，适合跟朋友外出喝酒，相对湿度65%-90%，有"辐射风"将在48小时内影响我市，请注意，这场台风将给我市吹来大量核辐射，请大家关好门窗，以防辐射污染

❏ （十）、1.天气预报说，最近几天没雨，大多是多云天气，所以很适合出门旅游或进行户外活动，我想明天去爬大南山，后天去大梅沙。欢迎你们跟我一起去 ◆ 2.在我们国家我喜欢秋季，因为我们国家秋季非常漂亮，气候也很好，可以去爬山。在深圳我喜欢夏季和秋季，因为夏天可以吃到荔枝，秋天的气候最舒服 ◆ 3.下雨的时候我心情不好，所以我喜欢在家睡觉。如果是晴天我喜欢出去散步，和朋友一起出去玩儿。如果在北方下雪的时候最好玩，我会和朋友一起玩儿打雪仗

第二课：你家真漂亮！

❏ 根据课文回答问题：1.艾美丽喜欢喝乌龙茶 ◆ 2.会，吴帅会拉二胡 ◆ 3.会，艾美丽会弹钢琴 ◆ 4.吴帅和一个朋友一起住 ◆ 5.吴帅一般去超市买东西 ◆ 6."请别送我了，回去吧，"表示客气

❏（一）、去过北京、上海 ◆ 过得不错、很好 ◆ 弹钢琴、吉他 ◆ 拉二胡、小提琴 ◆ 修自行车、电脑 ◆ 在游泳、唱歌
❏（二）、1、特别 ◆ 2.参观 ◆ 3.遗憾 ◆ 4.款待 ◆ 5.水平 ◆ 6.留步 ◆ 7.谦虚 ◆ 8.听说
1. 以前 ◆ 2.本来 ◆ 3.等……再 ◆ 4.一般 ◆ 5.哪里
❏（三）、1.我一般上午九点去学校 ◆ 2.我觉得他很谦虚/我觉得他太谦虚了 ◆ 3.听说他生病了 ◆ 4.那我们去其它餐厅吃吧 ◆ 5.真遗憾啊
❏（四）、1.等雨停了我们再出门吧 ◆ 2.等考完了我们再去玩儿吧 ◆ 3.等病好了再去打球吧 ◆ 4.等有空儿了再去朋友家吧
1. 我一般每天八点上课 ◆ 2.我一般每天在学校的餐厅吃饭 ◆ 3.我一般每周打三次球 ◆ 4.我一般每天早上喝咖啡 ◆ 1.本来写对了，但改错了 ◆ 2.本来准备得很好，但考得不好 ◆ 3.本来想去银行取钱，但银行关门了 ◆ 4.本来想上车，但车开走了
❏（五）、拉——大提琴 ◆ 二胡；弹——钢琴 ◆ 琵琶；打——太极拳 排球 乒乓球；踢——足球
❏（六）、1.A句中的"还是"，表示选择疑问。B句中的"还是"表示确定选择 ◆ 2.表示在原来或已有的情况下，加上什么，或继续做什么 ◆ 3.表示到说话时为止，仍然保持或存在某种情况、状态 ◆ 4.表示在原来或已有的情况下，加上什么，或继续做什么 ◆ 5."还没……呢"表示到说话时为止，仍然没出现或不存在某情况
❏（七）、你真漂亮！——哪里哪里 ◆ 你汉语说得怎么样？—— 马马虎虎 ◆ 你今天过得怎么样？——很开心 ◆ 慢走！——请留步
❏（八）、略
❏（九）、1.在我们的国家，去朋友家做客一般送茶叶和酒，要注意座位的次序和礼貌 ◆ 2.我喜欢喝茶，我不喜欢喝可乐，因为喝茶对身体好，喝可乐容易长胖 ◆ 3.我的爱好是上网和运动。我也喜欢听音乐，我经常在周末的时候在学校篮球场一边打球一边听歌

第三课：你要租房子吗？

❏ 根据课文回答问题：1.想租一套离深圳大学近一点儿的房子 ◆ 2.一间卧室，一间客厅 ◆ 3.喜欢带阳台的房子 ◆ 4.月租金的一半 ◆ 5.先交一个月押金，以后每月月底交下一个月的租金。只要把钱存到房东给的银行帐户上就可以了
❏（一）、租 房、车 ◆ 月、年租 ◆ 中介公司、人员 ◆ 家电、家具齐全 ◆ 带阳台、电梯 ◆ 交房租、中介费
❏（二）、1.差不多 ◆ 2.算 ◆ 3.存 ◆ 4.商量 ◆ 5.方便 ◆ 6.联系 ◆ 7.稍微 8.装修 ◆ 1.房东 ◆ 2.房主 ◆ 3.房东 ◆ 4.房东
❏（三）、1.走路十五分钟 ◆ 2.我要跟家人商量一下儿 ◆ 3.算是会吧 ◆ 4.到时打电话就知道了 ◆ 5.买水果，另外买些零食
❏（四）、1.只要给他打个电话就可以了。只要租一套一房一厅的就可以了 ◆ 2.我的家离学校很远。宿舍离超市很近 ◆ 3.这件衣服很便宜，差不多六十块。走路就可以，差不多十分钟 ◆ 4.我不知道去哪儿看电影好，我要跟男朋友商量一下儿。我不知道在哪儿租房好，我回家跟家人商量一下儿 ◆ 5.我经常跟朋友用短信联系。我经常跟妈妈用电子邮件（E_mail）联系 ◆ 6.她漂亮是漂亮，就是性格不太好。他人好是好，就是太穷了
❏（五）、1.从上往下的意思 ◆ 2.结束工作或学习等 ◆ 3.放在动词后表示结果 ◆ 4.表示前后顺序或即将到来的意思 ◆ 5.表示动作短促 ◆ 6.表示前后顺序或即将到来的意思 ◆ 7.指某东西的下面，表处所 ◆ 8.表示降落 ◆ 9.表示低于某种程度
❏（六）、1.差不多三点五十分了 ◆ 2.两件衣服的款式差不多 ◆ 3.坐公交车的时间和坐出租差不多 ◆ 4."太"字和"大"字差不多 ◆ 1.裙子是很漂亮，就是太贵了 ◆ 2.房子是不错，就是离学校太远了 ◆ 3.汉语是很有意思，就是太难了 ◆ 4.天气是很晴朗，就是风太大了 ◆ 1.从你家到学校不算远。/从你家到学校算比较近 ◆ 2.原价230元，打折后200元，不算便宜。/原价230

元，打折后200元，算是便宜点儿 ◆ 3.他算是我的老师。/他算是我朋友 ◆ 4.学了一年钢琴，算会一点儿

☐（七）、1.略

2. 我想租芳华苑的那一套，南苑新村那套租金2000块有点儿贵，另外，我一个人住，一房一厅就可以了

☐（八）、1.我住在留学生楼，很方便，上课很近 ◆ 2.我住的是一房一厅的房子，房子不太大，但是朝阳的，也有阳台，我很喜欢。我们的小区很漂亮。楼下有公共汽车，上课来学校很方便 ◆ 3.我的房间很大，什么都有。家电有：电视、电脑、冰箱、空调、洗衣机、微波炉、烤箱、饮水机等。家具有：单人床、双人床、大衣柜、书柜、写字台、电视柜、沙发、茶几、餐桌、餐椅等

☐（九）、略

第四课：能不能便宜点儿？

☐ 根据课文回答问题：1.艾美丽155元买下来了 ◆ 2.他建议艾美丽多买一件，艾美丽没买 ◆ 3.艾美丽知道这件衣服的成本，明白店主卖得太贵了 ◆ 4.因为她的朋友买了一样的才140元 ◆ 5.是的，她很厉害

☐（一）、加价、水 ◆ 骗人、钱 ◆ 最多、好 ◆ 贵、难看死了 ◆ 欢迎光临 ◆ 讨价还价

☐（二）、◆ 1.死了 ◆ 2.算了 ◆ 3.要不 ◆ 4.怎么 ◆ 5.好了 ◆ 6.再 ◆ 7.才 ◆ 8.都
1.成本 ◆ 2.加 ◆ 3.以为 ◆ 4.厉害 ◆ 5.甩卖 ◆ 6.骗 ◆ 7.店主 ◆ 8.生意 ◆ 9.赚 ◆ 10.赔 ◆ 11.光临

☐（三）、1.那就打的算了 ◆ 2.都12点了 ◆ 3.最多70平方米 ◆ 4.我才学了一个月 ◆ 5.要不明天问老师？ ◆ 6.肯定不是我写的，我怎么可能写得这么好 ◆ 7.他很厉害，拉得很好 ◆ 8.今天热死了

☐（四）、1.怎么，今天才26度？ ◆ 2.怎么东西这么贵？ ◆ 3.怎么，有考试？ ◆ 4.一个小时怎么做得完？ ◆ 1.要不买一件红色的裙子？ ◆ 2.要不去吃四川菜？ ◆ 3.要不去看医生？ ◆ 4.要不你先走？ ◆ 1.这个东西太便宜了，才1块！ ◆ 2.时间太短了，才5分钟！ ◆ 3.它们距离非常近，才1km！ ◆ 4.今天气温太低了，才5度！ ◆ 1.从你的家到学校最多需要40分钟 ◆ 2.我朋友买的衣服最多300元 ◆ 3.她最多34岁 ◆ 4.我最多在中国住两年

☐（五）、一家饭馆 ◆ 一条裤子 ◆ 一杯 咖啡 ◆ 一间 卧室 ◆ 一位老师 ◆ 一件衣服 ◆ 一把吉他 ◆ 一种水果 ◆ 一块钱 ◆ 一张票 ◆ 一瓶酒 ◆ 一套房

☐（六）、（七）、（八）、略

☐（九）、1.我会讨价还价，最好的方法就是你不满意就走，买东西的人就会让你回来。还有就是说东西有问题、不好 ◆ 2.我刚来中国看到商店上写着7折，以为是便宜70%，原来是便宜30%，交钱时才发现错了

第五课：我房间的水龙头坏了

☐ 根据课文回答问题：1. 水龙头漏水 ◆ 2. 他换了一个新的水龙头 ◆ 3. 因为保修要凭收据 ◆ 4. 没有。要找生产厂家的专业人员 ◆ 5. 保修卡上有

☐（一）、帮你、同学 ◆ 漏水、雨 ◆ 数数、钱 ◆ 敲门、桌子 ◆ 检查身体、工作 ◆ 保存礼物、收据 ◆ 生产厂家 ◆ 专业人员 ◆ 售后服务务

☐（二）1. 检查 ◆ 2. 正好 ◆ 3. 马上 ◆ 4. 总是 ◆ 5. 意思 ◆ 6. 保存 ◆ 1.保修 维修 ◆ 2.维修 ◆ 3.报修 ◆ 4.保修

☐（三）、◆ 1. 该吃午饭了（该下课了） ◆ 2.三十分钟以内 ◆ 3. 我在路上，马上就到 ◆ 4.因为公司派我去学习 ◆ 6. 凭学生证才可以

☐（四）、1.人太多了，上不去车 ◆ 2.汉语不难，学得会 ◆ 3.饭太多了，吃不完 ◆ 4.字太小，看不见 ◆ 5.老师说的话听不懂

☐（五）、1. 有趣、好玩儿的意思 ◆ 2. 与"不好"一起表示"对不起"的意思 ◆ 3. 有趣、好

玩儿的意思 ◆ 4.表示字句或某些事物的含义
☐（六）、派人 ◆ 凭票 ◆ 数钱 ◆ 漏水 ◆ 免费 ◆ 敲门
☐（七）、◆ 1.该上课了了 ◆ 2.该去银行了 ◆ 3.该买短袖了 ◆ 4.该穿大衣了 ◆ 1. 300元以内我就买 ◆ 2.一分钟以内写65个字 ◆ 3. 3公里以内12.5元 ◆ 4.三个人以内可以
☐（八）、1. A:你好！是售后服务部吗？B:对，您有什么事？A:我的热水器打不着了 B:请问您的热水器什么时候买的？A:我记不清了，大概半年多吧 B:你有保修单和发票吗？A:有 B:那好，我们派师傅去给您看一下儿 A:好的，谢谢。我住在深圳大学留学生楼239房间 ◆ 2. A:您好，请问：是海尔空调维修部吗？B:对，有什么可以帮到您？A:我的空调不制冷了 B:请问：您的空调还在保修期以内吗？B:我记不清了，有五年了吧 A:那已经过了保修期。如果维修，是要收费的 B:没问题 A:那好，明天下午三点去给您修，我们会有师傅跟您联系 B:好的，谢谢！ ◆ 3. A:你好，先生。我的钥匙忘在房间里了 B:你再仔细找一找 A:我都找了，没有。是忘在房间里了 B:那我去找个师傅来帮你把门打开 A:好的，谢谢！ ◆ 4. A:服务员你好！我洗手间的下水道堵了 B:你住哪个房间？A:我住509房间 B:那好，我马上派人去给你看一下。请先不要用卫生间了 A:好的，谢谢！
☐（九）、1.我刚来中国的时候，我的空调坏了，我打电话给维修的人，那个人说："请等一下儿，我马上到"。我以为两三分钟以后他就到了，可是最后等了一个多小时才到。从那时起我知道了，中国人说马上是很长时间的意思 ◆ 2.我觉得修比较好，因为买比较麻烦，也很贵，扔了也不环保。特别是空调等大的家电。但是，如果一件东西用的时间太长了，修了也用不了多长时间，那就还是买新的吧 ◆ 3.应该先找商店，商店会帮我们找厂家

第六课：你要什么新发型？

☐ 根据课文回答问题：1.吴帅觉得艾美丽染什么颜色头发都好看 ◆ 2.因为艾美丽的头发分叉了，所以她想去保养她的头发 ◆ 3.吴帅喜欢艾美丽留长头发的样子 ◆ 4.艾美丽要的是普通的洗发水 ◆ 5.头发剪短以后显得更精神了
☐（一）、海、水边 ◆ 饭、理发店 ◆ 洗头发、衣服 ◆ 更好、快 ◆ 顾客满意 ◆ 效果显著 ◆ 保养皮肤
☐（二）、产品 失望 满意 顺便 精神 优惠 普通 样子 ◆ 刚刚 刚才 刚才 ◆ 最 更 最 更
☐（三）、1.他正在写作业呢 ◆ 2.我刚去图书馆了 ◆ 3.但看起来还很年轻 ◆ 4.我们让修理工帮你修理一下吧 ◆ 5.我觉得你穿这条裙子显得你的身材更好了
☐（四）、皮肤 白 ◆ 头发 开叉 ◆ 留 短发 ◆ 照 镜子 ◆ 染 颜色
☐（五）、略
☐（六）、染头发。我想去染头发，你觉得怎么样呢？ ◆ 吹头发。我刚洗完头，正在吹头发呢 ◆ 剪头发。我不舍得剪头发，好不容易才留长的 ◆ 烫头发。我想去烫头发，这样显得成熟一点 ◆ 洗头发。在理发店洗头发好贵啊 ◆ 焗头发。你的头发分叉了，我建议你去焗头发 ◆ 留头发。夏天到了，我想留头发，这样穿裙子会很好看
☐（七）、1.染头发，洗头发，烫头发，焗油，护理，剪头发 ◆ 2.洗发水，梳子，护发素，焗油膏，染发剂
☐（八）、略
☐（九）、1.我留过很多种发型，长发、短发、直发、卷发。我最喜欢短发，我觉得短发很精神，运动时也方便 ◆ 2.很重要。它可以表现出一个人的状态和气质

第七课：我们去听音乐会吧

☐ 根据课文回答问题：1."七夕"是中国的情人节 ◆ 2.吴帅和艾美丽去听音乐会 ◆ 3.吴帅和艾美丽约好在地铁站见面 ◆ 4.因为路上塞车了 ◆ 5.她没有生气
☐（一）、掏手机、门票 ◆ 订演出票、机票 ◆ 开始表演、唱歌 ◆ 了解我、中国文化 ◆ 不见不散 ◆ 塞车高峰期

☐（二）、1、正常 ◆ 2、迟到 ◆ 3、路上 ◆ 4、严重 ◆ 5、主意 ◆ 6、了解 ◆ 7、担心 ◆ 8、生气 ◆ 9、原谅

☐（三）、
1. 我打算去吃饭 ◆ 2. 谁说的？我拉得不好 ◆ 3. 我有一个好主意，我们去爬山吧 ◆ 4. 好的，不见不散 ◆ 5. 别紧张，还来得及 ◆ 6. 别担心，他很快就回来了 ◆ 7. 别提了，我的手机丢了 ◆ 8. 他生气了

☐（四）、1. 就 ◆ 2. 才 ◆ 3. 才 ◆ 4. 就 ◆ 5. 就，才 ◆ 6. 才

☐（五）、长—短 ◆ 早—晚 ◆ 便宜—贵 ◆ 好——坏 ◆ 真——假 ◆ 新——旧 ◆ 赔——赚

☐（六）、2. 3. 5. 6. 4. 1.

☐（七）、1. A:阿里，你的飞机大概几点到？B:大概三点到 A:那好，我去机场接你。我在机场的旅客出口处等你 B:好的。不见不散 ◆ 2. A:田中，星期五下午3点我们一起去沃尔玛买东西好不好？B:不好意思，星期五下午3点我约了朋友一起去打球 A:那你什么时候有时间？B:星期六怎么样？A:可以。我们几点见面呢？B:上午10点怎么样？A:好，那就星期六上午10点。我去你的宿舍找你，我们一起走好吗？B:好的。星期六见 A:星期六见！ ◆ 3. A:我最近发现了一家不错的餐厅，哪天我们一起去好不好？B:好啊，什么时候去？A:那你什么时候有时间？B:我什么时候都有时间，看你方便吧 A:那我们这个星期天去怎么样？听说海岸城的滑冰场开放了，我们吃饭以后还可以去滑冰 B:那太好了！A:那星期天上午11点。我在深大正门等你 B:好的。星期天11点见 A:星期天见！

☐（八）、A:这几天百老汇影城在演《致命伴侣》，我们一起去看吧 B:好啊，我正想去看呢 A:明天下午你有时间吗？B:我下午有课，4点半以后可以 A:那我们看下午5点15的吧 B:好啊 A:4点半我们在图书馆门口见面怎么样？B:好的。明天下午见 A:明天见！

☐（九）、1. 我很喜欢旅游，我觉得旅游很有意思。特别是在中国旅游。不仅可以看到中国的很多好玩的地方，还可以和中国人聊天、说汉语。我的女朋友不喜欢旅游，她喜欢唱歌、跳舞。可我觉得唱歌跳舞没意思，所以我常常一个人去旅游。不过我有时也会陪她去唱歌、跳舞，因为如果我不去，她会生气的 ◆ 2. 我看玛丽最近心情不好，我问她为什么她也不说，后来听她的同屋说，她妈妈最近生病了，她很担心，很想回国去看妈妈，可妈妈怕影响她学习，不让她回去，所以她常常想家，想妈妈

第八课：吃哪种药好得快？

☐ 根据课文回答问题：1. 艾美丽感冒了，鼻塞，嗓子不舒服，头也疼 ◆ 2. "犯困"就是想睡觉 ◆ 3. 艾美丽发烧了，38度 ◆ 4. 没有 ◆ 5. 多喝水，多休息

☐（一）、取药、钱 ◆ 胃、喉咙疼 ◆ 开饭、药 ◆ 吃、喝药 ◆ 输液、送 ◆ 喝、倒水 ◆ 犯、病困 ◆ 化验、考试结果

☐（二）、1.考试 ◆ 2.结果 ◆ 3.效果 ◆ 4.休息 ◆ 5.感冒 ◆ 6.过敏 ◆ 7.说明 ◆ 8.化验

☐（三）、1. 说明书上有 ◆ 2. 一开始很难，现在还好 ◆ 3. 一开始不习惯，现在习惯了 ◆ 4. 他胃疼得来不了了 ◆ 5. 一盒三九感冒灵

☐（四）、1.写出 ◆ 2.营业 ◆ 3.打开 ◆ 4.写出 ◆ 5.加热到100度 ◆ 6.驾驶

☐（五）、消炎 ◆ 取药 ◆ 发烧 ◆ 张嘴 ◆ 输液 ◆ 验血 ◆ 打针

☐（六）、1. 拉肚子，呕吐、发烧 ◆ 2. 头疼、嗓子疼、咳嗽、发烧、鼻塞、流鼻涕 ◆ 3. 起红疙瘩、皮肤痒 ◆ 4. 红肿、有青紫色瘀伤、皮肤擦伤、出血

☐（七）、1. 你去不去深圳大学？ ◆ 2. 你是不是深圳大学的学生？ ◆ 3. 你学没学过汉语？ ◆ 4. 你喜不喜欢打太极拳？ ◆ 5. 现在去来得及来不及？ ◆ 6 你明天上不上课？ ◆ 7. 你愿不愿意教我汉语？ ◆ 8. 可不可以坐公交车去深圳机场？

☐（八）、略

❏（九）、

请假条

尊敬的老师：

    你好！我今天发烧38度，头疼、咳嗽，不能去上课了，特此向老师请假。请老师批准。

    此致，

敬礼！

艾美丽
2011 .4.15

❏（十）、1. 来中国以后我得了肠胃炎，拉肚子、呕吐，还发烧。原来我吃了路边小摊的烤羊肉串，因为不干净，所以吃了以后拉肚子了。在中国，去医院最大的问题是不会说汉语，医生说的话我也听不懂，所以生病的时候很害怕，也很想家 ◆ 2. 不太了解。我只去过一次医院，觉得中国的医院人很多。在我们国家看病有时要提前预约，一般情况人比较少 ◆ 3. 我见过中医看病，医生把手放在病人的手腕上摸几下儿，再看看病人的舌头。还有的医生用很细的针扎在病人的手上或者身上。中医开的药都是很多树根、树皮等植物，把这些树根、树皮放在一起煮，然后喝煮好的汤，很苦。我们国家也有中医

第九课：我最喜欢大熊猫了

❏ 根据课文回答问题：1. 簕杜鹃 ◆ 2.榕树 ◆ 3.熊猫 ◆ 4.国宝 ◆ 5.没有 ◆ 6.她就想家了

❏（一）、泡脚、茶 ◆ 养宠物、花 ◆ 长胡子、痘痘 ◆ 想家、睡觉

❏（二）、◆ 1.其实 ◆ 2.从来 ◆ 3.怪不得 ◆ 4.称，是 ◆ 5.比较 ◆ 6.却 ◆ 1.但是\却 ◆ 2.却 ◆ 3.但是 ◆ 4.却

❏（三）、1.喜欢。它看起来很可爱 ◆ 2.怪不得他不来上课 ◆ 3.我有一位中国朋友却很讨厌红色 ◆ 4.我从来不染头发 ◆ 5.是的，他平时很喜欢开玩笑 ◆ 6.不是，其实我们只是见过几次

❏（四）、耳朵 ◆ 眼睛 ◆ 嘴巴 ◆ 鼻子 看 ◆ 说 ◆ 听 ◆ 闻

❏（五）、鼠、牛、虎、兔、龙、蛇、马、羊、猴、鸡、狗、猪 ◆ 鼠：眼睛小小的，尾巴长长的 牛：个子和眼睛都大大的，有两只长长的角 ◆ 虎：额头有一个"王"字。老虎有一对大大的牙齿。

兔：白白的毛，红红的眼睛 ◆ 龙：在画上看过，眼睛大大的，尾巴长长的 ◆ 蛇：身体细细的、长长的，有的蛇是有毒的，很危险 ◆ 马：个子高高的，力气很大，跑得很快 ◆ 羊：毛白白的，尾巴短短的，很温顺的样子 ◆ 猴：很聪明，爬得很高、很快，屁股红红的 ◆ 鸡：天亮就会叫，头上有一个红红的鸡冠，很漂亮 ◆ 狗：是人类的朋友，会看家。天气热的时候会伸出长长的舌头 ◆ 猪：头大大的，尾巴小小的，身体胖胖的

❏（六）、我喜欢兔子，因为她很听话，而且红耳朵、红眼睛，看上去很漂亮、可爱。我讨厌猫，因为我小时候养了一只小鸟，后来被猫吃了，我很难过，所以从此以后就不喜欢猫了 ◆ 我喜欢勒杜鹃，因为她的颜色非常鲜艳、漂亮。我不喜欢月季花，因为它有刺

❏（七）、1.兰花 ◆ 2.蒲公英 ◆ 3.菊花 ◆ 4.玫瑰 ◆ 5.榕树 ◆ 6.松树 ◆ 7.竹子 ◆ 8.柳树 ◆ 9.牡丹 ◆ 10.梅花 ◆ 11.茉莉 ◆ 12.康乃馨

❏（八）、1. 我养过一只鹦鹉，牠很有意思，牠可以学人说话，可是有一天下雨的时候我把鸟笼子放在外面了，结果第二天牠就死了。我很难过 ◆ 2. 我们日本的国花是樱花，樱花在春天的时候开，非常漂亮

❏（九）、1.大象 ◆ 2.公鸡 ◆ 3.狗 ◆ 4.羊 ◆ 5.鱼 ◆ 6.蟹 ◆ 7.猫 ◆ 8.蛇 ◆ 9.猴子 ◆ 10.熊猫 ◆ 11.鹅 ◆ 12.兔子 ◆ 13.老虎 ◆ 14.牛 ◆ 15.孔雀 ◆ 谜语答案：1.梅花、莓、杨梅、桃、虾（瞎）、对虾（对瞎）、龙虾（聋瞎） ◆ 2.松树3.竹子4.柳树5,兰花、6牡丹7.蒲公英8.梅花

第十课：我们一起出去庆祝一下吧！

❏ 根据课文回答问题：1. 同学们建议艾美丽去海岸城的KTV ◆ 2.免费赠送一盘水果，一支香槟。同时，还免费给艾美丽办理一张会员卡 ◆ 3.因为那里不但有很多经典歌曲和流行歌曲，还有不少英文歌 ◆ 4.艾美丽说：虽然我不会喝酒，但是今天一定要喝。因为我听说中国人开心的时候喝酒喜欢不醉不归 ◆ 5.《月亮代表我的心》 ◆ 6.意思是不喝醉就不回家，是喝得尽兴的意思

❏ （一）、举杯、手 ◆ 流行歌曲、语 ◆ 喝酒、茶 ◆ 复习生词、课文 ◆ 娱乐场所、活动 ◆ 价格合理、便宜 ◆ 不醉不归

❏ （二）、1.环境 ◆ 2.享受 ◆ 3.庆祝 ◆ 4.赠送 ◆ 5.流行 ◆ 6.合理 ◆ 7.场所 ◆ 8.参加 ◆

1.平时 ◆ 2.为了 ◆ 3.一定 ◆ 4.来着 ◆ 5.光 ◆ 6.同时

❏ （三）、1.深圳夏天的天气不但很热，而且经常下大雨 ◆ 2.昨天我们去的那家饭馆叫什么名字来着？ ◆ 3.虽然我不喜欢你，但是你需要我的帮助 ◆ 4.如果你有会员卡就可以便宜点儿 ◆ 5.为上课方便点儿

❏ （四）、1.东门的衣服不但价格便宜而且款式很好 ◆ 2.如果你有困难就打电话告诉我 ◆ 3.虽然这件衣服很漂亮，但是太贵了 ◆ 4.他来深圳已经八年了，所以对深圳很熟悉

❏ （五）、一条围巾 ◆ 一首歌 ◆ 一打啤酒 ◆ 一朵花 ◆ 一粒药 ◆ 一棵树 ◆ 一盘水果 ◆ 一只猫

❏ （六）、1.是"正确"的意思 ◆ 2."忽然想起来了"的意思 ◆ 3.表示相反、相比、相关的关系。词句是"……兑换成……"的意思 ◆ 4.表示人、事物、行为之间的对待关系 ◆ 5.表示人、事物、行为之间的对待关系 ◆ 6.表示相反、相比、相关的关系。此句是"配合"、"合作"的意思

❏ （七）、我选择周一——周五白天场的VIP房。我觉得这个价钱比较便宜，而且适合我们这些白天不工作的人。我想VIP房的音响效果可能比较好，所以我选择VIP房

❏ （八）、略

❏ （九）、1. 我和朋友在一起吃饭、吹蜡烛、吃蛋糕，一起唱《祝你生日快乐》。我觉得这样很喜庆、热闹。而且可以和朋友聚聚，增进友谊！ ◆ 2. 我会根据朋友的特点，猜想朋友可能会喜欢什么，然后送给朋友喜欢的东西。如果没有特别的，就送鲜花或蛋糕 ◆ 3. 离深圳大学比较近的海岸城是休闲娱乐的好地方，在那里吃饭、购物、唱歌、看电影等等都很方便

第十一课：深圳是个什么样的城市？

❏ 根据课文回答问题：1. 美善羡慕艾美丽的汉语进步很大 ◆ 2. 深圳外国人很多，他们来学汉语，也有很多人来投资 ◆ 3. 深圳大部分人说普通话 ◆ 4．艾美丽非常喜欢逛街 ◆ 5. 善美担心来深圳不习惯吃中国菜 ◆ 6. 世界之窗、锦绣中华、欢乐谷 ◆ 7. 听艾美丽介绍以后美善觉得深圳很好，现在就想去 ◆ 8. 艾美丽觉得深圳虽然历史不长，但是很发达，既漂亮又繁华

❏ （一）、回国、家 ◆ 参观博物馆、风景名胜 ◆ 工作、购物狂 ◆ 吸引外国人、我的朋友 ◆ 购物广场、街 ◆ 一言为定

❏ （二）、1. 历史 ◆ 2.好玩 ◆ 3. 风味 ◆ 4. 决定 ◆ 5. 发达 ◆ 6. 怀念 ◆ 7. 投资 ◆ 8．羡慕

❏ （三）、1. 既香又辣 ◆ 2. 我打算去逛街，另外去电影院看电影 ◆ 3. 我不仅去过，而且还去了好几次了 ◆ 4. 恐怕去不了，我要带我的朋友去看病 ◆ 5．他们来自很多国家，像韩国、日本、俄罗斯、土耳其、美国等 ◆ 6. 我还没决定。/我决定后天回国 ◆ 7. 我的汉语进步很大 ◆ 8. 因为他是个吸引人的老师。/因为他讲课很吸引人

❏ （四）、1.听你这么说，我都不想学了 ◆ 2.听老师这么说我很紧张 ◆ 3.听朋友这么说我现在就想去 ◆ 4. 听朋友这么说我很感动。/听朋友这么说我都饿了 ◆ 1.别看他上去很年轻，其实他已经六十岁了 ◆ 2.别看他汉语很好，但他依然每天努力学习 ◆ 3.别看他不戴眼镜，其实

他眼睛近视。/别看他没戴眼镜，其实他戴了隐形眼镜 ◆ 4.别看这道菜只有两种东西，其实很难做 ◆ 1.书店有各种各样的书，想看/读什么都有 ◆ 2．饭馆有各种风味的菜，想吃什么都有 ◆ 3．娱乐场所有各种好玩的，想玩什么都有 ◆ 4．家里有很多DVD，想看什么都有 ◆ 1.回家太晚，恐怕没有公交车坐了 ◆ 2.时间太短，恐怕写不完试卷了 ◆ 3.天气不好，恐怕不能去野餐了 ◆ 4.有急事儿，恐怕我要先走了

☐（五）、移民城市 ◆ 上网聊天 ◆ 吸引客人 ◆ 风味餐厅 ◆ 参观景点 ◆ 全国各地 ◆ 怀念朋友

☐（六）、1．表示问候的意思 ◆ 2．令人满意的意思 ◆ 3．看上去觉得满意 ◆ 4．吃起来觉得满意 ◆ 5．表示动作完成的意思 ◆ 6．问对方是否满意、同意 ◆ 7．玩儿起来觉得满意 ◆ 8．身体痊愈的意思

☐（七）、"深圳速度"是中国大陆形容建设速度非常快的一个词。这个词出自1982年11月～1985年12月的37个月期间，中国的一家建筑公司在建深圳国际贸易中心大厦（简称国贸大厦）时，三天盖一层楼，这在当时的中国是没有的。因此"深圳速度"、"三天一层楼"是当时媒体提到深圳常用的词汇

☐（八）、锦绣中华——中华民俗村是深圳有名的旅游景点，这个景点很有中国特色，你可以在那里了解很多中国文化，特别是少数民族文化。深圳有全世界、全中国的美食，在深圳你可以吃到各种美食。深圳买东西也很方便，有很多大型的购物广场。深圳是个移民城市，因此不同人群的风俗习惯也不一样，另外，深圳离香港很近，受香港影响也很大，很多西方的节日深圳人也都过。我去过欢乐谷，觉得很好，特别适合年轻人玩儿，很多游乐设施很刺激。

☐（九）、1.我觉得深圳年轻人很多，城市很有活力 ◆ 2.我去过深圳的很多地方，像：世界之窗、锦绣中华——中华民俗村、欢乐谷、华强北等，我最喜欢欢乐谷 ◆ 3.我住的城市很小，人也很少，很安静，也很干净，但有时会觉得有点儿无聊，我喜欢热闹的地方，所以我喜欢深圳

第十二课：路上辛苦了！

☐ 根据课文回答问题：1．因为发生了交通事故 ◆ 2．他们没有迟到 ◆ 3．美善坐的航班晚了半个小时 ◆ 4．美善以前没见过吴帅 ◆ 5．美善觉得吴帅长得很帅 ◆ 6．不担心

☐（一）、吃饭、醋 ◆ 算账、钱 ◆ 挥手、围巾 ◆ 航班晚点、号 ◆ 发生事故、事情

☐（二）、1.夸奖 ◆ 2.善良 ◆ 3.事故 ◆ 4.晚点 ◆ 5.配 ◆ 6.终于 ◆ 7.介绍 ◆ 8.办法

☐（三）、1.那我只好找别人和我去听音乐会了 ◆ 2.对不起，我光顾着学习汉语了 ◆ 3.最近身体很糟糕 ◆ 4.还好，已经慢慢习惯了 ◆ 5.我今天有事，改天再说吧 ◆ 6.她吃小张的醋了 ◆ 7．我在上课呢。◆ 8.等回家再跟你算账

☐（四）、1.你要来深圳的话，我去接你 ◆ 2.身体不好的话，要休息 ◆ 3.有问题的话，可以问老师 ◆ 4.堵车的话会迟到 ◆ 1.你要好好休息，不然明天考试没精神 ◆ 2.你一定要来，不然大家就不去了 ◆ 3.下雨了，要带伞，不然就淋湿了 ◆ 4.不要喝那么多酒，不-然对身体不好 ◆ 1.要迟到了，还不快走 ◆ 2.发烧了，还不快去医院 ◆ 3.明天有考试，还不快复习 ◆ 4.头发太长了，还不快去剪

☐（五）、1.秋天就要过去了，天气慢慢地冷了 ◆ 2.情人节就要来了，买支玫瑰花给女朋友吧 ◆ 3.台风就要来了，把衣服收起来吧 ◆ 4.老师就要来了，准备上课吧 ◆ 1.难道你不知道这件事？◆ 2.难道你不喜欢这首歌？◆ 3.难道你们认识？◆ 4.难道你的话是真的？◆ 1.今天没带雨伞，倒下雨了 ◆ 2.他不是四川人，倒比四川人喜欢吃辣的 ◆ 3.平时不堵车，星期天倒堵车 ◆ 4.考试没准备，考得倒挺好 ◆ 1.我得早点儿休息 ◆ 2.朋友来了，得去机场接 ◆ 3.感冒了，得去医院看病 ◆ 4.在家请客，得去超市买菜。

☐（六）、菜很多--吃不完 ◆ 很久没见面--认不出 ◆ 时间太短了--来不及 ◆ 天很黑一看不见 ◆ 忘了东西在哪儿—找不到

☐（七）、我有一个好朋友叫汤姆，他很善良，人长得也很帅，就有点儿小心眼儿，喜欢听人夸奖，比较容易吃醋

☐（八）、A:玛丽！我在这儿！B:小美，我们又见面了！◆ A:路上辛苦了！B:飞机晚点了，让你久

等了 ◆ A:没关系。路上塞车,我也是刚到 B:我们现在去哪儿? ◆ A:我们先去吃饭,我已经订好了,吃完饭再回酒店 B:好的,谢谢!
☐（九）、1. 我觉得深圳的交通有点儿拥挤,上下班的时候很容易堵车,有一回我下午下班回家,塞车塞了两个小时,回到家都晚上九点了。平时的话,交通还可以 ◆ 2. 如果我是深圳市市长,我会多建立交桥,增加公交车的数量,建城市轻轨

第十三课：我想在深圳找工作

☐ 根据课文回答问题：1. 不是。她想在深圳找工作 ◆ 2. 跟经济管理有关的工作 ◆ 3. 1999年从美国长岛大学本科毕业,取得了经济学学士学位 ◆ 4. 财政主管 ◆ 5. 平均月收入一万元
☐（一）、当经理、老师 ◆ 管理、经济学 ◆ 财务、经济管理 ◆ 提供午餐、条件
☐（二）、◆ 1.招聘 ◆ 2.推荐 ◆ 3.是否 ◆ 4.简单 ◆ 5.经济 ◆ 6.继续 ◆ 7.能力 ◆ 8.胜任
☐（三）、1.可能跟他的女朋友有关 ◆ 2.我是否能参加这次活动? ◆ 3.让小王自己跟你说吧 ◆ 4.我以前当过英语老师 ◆ 5.平均每周两次
☐（四）、经济管理 ◆ 学士学位 ◆ 拨通电话 ◆ 提供岗位 ◆ 本科毕业 ◆ 经验丰富
☐（五）、1. 我2005年9月至1月在深圳大学学汉语。我上午8点半至11点50在学校上课 ◆ 2. 你是否喜欢学汉语?你是否想在深圳工作? ◆ 3. 身体好坏跟生活习惯有关。东西的价钱跟质量有关。
☐（六）、×××,女,1984年10月生于莫斯科,2002年至2006年在莫斯科大学学习经济管理专业,2007年4月至2010年5月在一家公司做职员。2010年3月来到中国,在深圳大学学汉语。我希望今后做跟汉语有关的工作
☐（七）、A:你好!请问你的专业是什么? B:我学的是心理学专业 ◆ A:可我们招聘的岗位是人事管理,你觉得你能胜任吗? B:我觉得我能。因为人事管理最重要的是人,管理人最重要的是了解一个人的心,所以我觉得我的专业会对我的工作有帮助 ◆ A:你在国外工作过吗? B:我在英国工作过两年 ◆ A:好的,今天先谈到这里,我们商量后给你消息 B:好的,谢谢!
☐（八）、1. 理发师 ◆ 2. 木匠 ◆ 3. 铁匠
☐（九）、1. 在我的国家找工作比较难,我来中国以前在我爸爸的公司工作,但我不喜欢那份工作,所以我来中国学汉语,我希望在中国找到我喜欢的工作 ◆ 2. 在我的国家医生的职业比较受欢迎,薪水很高,也很受人尊重,但要当医生很难

第十四课：带什么礼物回国好?

☐ 根据课文回答问题：1. 因为艾美丽要回国了,她想带点儿礼物给家人和朋友 ◆ 2.艾美丽觉得这些礼物太普通了 ◆ 3.艾美丽想送家人和朋友特别点儿的或者他们需要的以及既实用又有中国特色的礼物 ◆ 4. 因为中国的茶非常有名,而且茶很轻,好带 ◆ 5.课文中提到的工艺品有扇子、中国结、剪纸、泥人、脸谱 ◆ 6.艾美丽的同学送给艾美丽一幅中国画,因为艾美丽的爸爸喜欢中国画。这件礼物不是买的,是艾美丽同学的画家爷爷画的
☐（一）、看望朋友、父母 ◆ 爱好唱歌、运动 ◆ 实用的礼物 ◆ 有名的歌手 ◆ 普通的衣服
☐（二）、1. 普通 ◆ 2. 放假 ◆ 3. 实用 ◆ 4. 特色 ◆ 5. 爱好 ◆ 6. 有名 ◆ 7. 看望 ◆ 8. 未来 ◆ 1.或者 ◆ 2.还是 ◆ 3.还是 ◆ 4.或者
☐（三）、1.去海南岛或者夏威夷 ◆ 2.除了吃丰盛的晚餐还吃生日蛋糕 ◆ 3.快要考试了,我在复习 ◆ 4.她既美丽又温柔 ◆ 5.我要回国了,带点儿礼物回去
☐（四）、一个钱包 一份礼物 ◆ 一杯茶 一把扇子 ◆ 一幅画
☐（五）、1."阅读"、"观看"的意思 ◆ 2."觉得"、"认为"的意思 ◆ 3.在重叠动词后,表示尝试、试试的意思 ◆ 4."看望"的意思
☐（六）、A:周末我们去大梅沙或者南澳玩儿好吗? B:好啊!我觉得还是去大梅沙好 ◆ A:那好,我们就去大梅沙。B:只有我们两个人还是还有别人? ◆ A:我还没来得及跟别人说。B:再找几个人吧,人多有意思 ◆ A:那我们叫上张伟和麦克,让他们也带上他们的女朋友吧。B:好,我去给他们

打电话。你准备出游的东西 ◆ A:好，听你的
- （七）、1.扇子 ◆ 2.茶 ◆ 3.剪纸 ◆ 4.泥人 ◆ 5.书法 ◆ 6.中国画
- （八）、1．买一件毛衣送给妈妈 ◆ 买一个MP4送给侄女 ◆ 买一张电影的DVD送给朋友 ◆ 买一件新衣服给自己 ◆ 2.略
- （九）、1.我想买些茶叶，我的很多朋友喜欢喝中国茶。我还想买一些京剧脸谱和剪纸，因为它们很有中国特色 ◆ 2.我会送他一幅中国画，让他挂在他们的新房 ◆ 3.我会带我们国家的特产，比如：糖果、巧克力等。我们国家的糖果和巧克力很有名，吃起来口感很好，包装也很漂亮

第十五课：中国值得去的地方太多了

- 根据课文回答问题：1．西安 ◆ 2.秦始皇陵 ◆ 3.自助游，因为这样他们可以在自己喜欢的地方呆久点儿 ◆ 4.苏州，杭州，桂林，西安
- （一）、值得去、看 ◆ 安排 考试、旅游 ◆ 许多人、地方 ◆ 自助游、餐 ◆ 风土人情 ◆ 名胜古迹 ◆ 自然风光光
- （二）、1.古老 ◆ 2.发现 ◆ 3.值得 ◆ 4.联系 ◆ 5.许多 ◆ 6.安排 ◆ 7.一直 ◆ 8.俗语
- （三）、1.他最近一直在生病 ◆ 2你安排吧 ◆ 3.不过，值得，这儿的风景太美了！ ◆ 4.没有，我也很长时间没跟他联系了 ◆ 5.哪儿都没去，就在家呆着了
- （四）、1.天上最美的地方是天堂，地上（人间）最美的地方是苏州和杭州 ◆ 2.桂林山水是天下第一美丽的地方 ◆ 3.看完五座著名的山，回来后就不想再看别的山了，如果看了黄山，回来后就不想看"五岳"了。意思是黄山是最美的山
- （五）、园林：拙政园，狮子林，留园，沧浪亭 ◆ 自然风光： 西湖，黄山，漓江，庐山，太湖，泰山，三峡，九寨沟 ◆ 陵墓：秦始皇陵，明十三陵
- （六）、1.深圳有很多可去的地方 ◆ 2.商店有很多可买的东西 ◆ 3.我觉得跟他没什么可说的 ◆ 4.他有很多可学习的地方 ◆ 1.深圳很热，特别是夏天 ◆ 2.我喜欢运动，特别是打网球 ◆ 3.他喜欢看书，特别是旅游方面的书 ◆ 4.我觉得汉语很难，特别是汉字
- （七）、1.埃菲尔铁塔：埃菲尔铁塔（Eiffel Tower，法语：La Tour Eiffel）是一座于1889年建成位于法国巴黎的铁塔，高300米，天线高24米，总高324米。埃菲尔铁塔得名于设计它的桥梁工程师居斯塔夫·埃菲尔。铁塔设计新颖独特，是世界建筑史上的杰作，因而成为法国和巴黎的一个重要景点和突出标志。苏伊士运河（The Suez Canal），1859-1869年凿成。著名的国际通航运河。位于埃及境内，是连通欧亚非三大洲的主要国际海运航道，连接红海与地中海，使大西洋、地中海与印度洋联结起来，大大缩短了东西方航程。它是亚洲与非洲的分界线之一 ◆ 2.我喜欢昆明，那里气候好，夏天不需要空调，冬天不需要暖气，生活节奏慢，适合居住 ◆ 3.俗话说，上有天堂，下有苏杭。我一直想去杭州。今年暑假我去了。杭州真是一个值得去的旅游胜地，那儿不仅有很美丽的风景，而且有许多古老的寺庙和园林。另外，杭州近几年的经济发展也很快，所以杭州也是一个现代化的城市
- （八）、略
- （九）、1.我去过海南岛、桂林、云南。在桂林旅游的时候我认识了一个中国的大学生，我们在游船上认识的。一路上我们一起聊天、一起玩，他给我讲了很多跟中国文化有关的故事。最让我开心的是我们一起说汉语，我第一次用汉语跟中国人说了那么长时间的话，我觉得我的汉语在一天中进步了很多。这次旅游让我更喜欢学汉语了 ◆ 2.我喜欢去有海的地方旅游，因为我喜欢大海，也喜欢游泳

第十六课：祝你一路顺风！

- 根据课文回答问题：1．艾美丽在深圳呆了四年了 ◆ 2.艾美丽感谢同学们在四年里的照顾和关心，很舍不得离开 ◆ 3.这句话的意思是如果是朋友，不管相隔多远都像在身边一样 ◆ 4.因为艾美丽的男朋友吴帅在中国
- （一）、照顾 小孩、父母 ◆ 想念 家乡、亲人 ◆ 珍惜 时光、机会 ◆ 保持 冷静、距离

❏（二）、1.照顾 ◆ 2.保持 ◆ 3.珍惜 ◆ 4.保重 ◆ 5.情景 ◆ 6.害怕 ◆ 7.想念 ◆ 8.机会

❏（三）、1.请代我问候你的父母 ◆ 2.不好意思，我舍不得㊢ ◆ 3.我很珍惜在中国的这段时间。/这段时间值得珍惜 ◆ 4.有，我一直和王老师保持联系 ◆ 5.谢谢，你也要保重身体！ ◆ 6.我在照顾小孩 ◆ 7.他替生病的李老师上课 ◆ 8.我有点想念家乡

❏（四）、1.不管天气怎么样都要去旅游 ◆ 2.不管汉语有多难，都要学 ◆ 3.不管同学去不去，我都去 ◆ 4.不管什么菜我都喜欢 ◆ 1.同学们都知道这件事了，还用告诉大家吗？ ◆ 2.时间很多，还担心完不成工作吗？ ◆ 3.菜已经很多了，还用再买吗？ ◆ 4.大家都明白了，还需要再讲吗？ ◆ 1.你什么时候去我家？到时候我去接你 ◆ 2.如果去KTV，到时候我们一起唱歌 ◆ 3.如果你想学汉语，到时候可以跟我学 ◆ 4.你过生日的话到时候我请你吃饭 ◆ 1.他怎么会不来？ ◆ 2.他怎么会不喜欢你送的礼物？ ◆ 3.他怎么会知道这件事？ ◆ 4.这个字学过，怎么不会写呢？

❏（五）、保持---联系 ◆ 照顾---孩子 ◆ 保重---身体 ◆ 想念---家人 ◆ 珍惜---友谊

❏（六）、一段时光 ◆ 一首古诗 ◆ 一份工作 ◆ 一家公司

❏（七）、（八）、略

❏（九）、1．我去年来中国的时候，是爸爸送我到机场，那天下大雨，天气很冷，爸爸穿的衣服不多，那时候我很伤心，很舍不得走，但最后还是上了飞机，现在过节的时候就经常会想起亲人，想家 ◆ 2．刚来深圳的时候，很不习惯，生活方面有很多困难。但我身边的中国朋友们常常帮助我，真的很感谢他们。因为有了他们，我在中国的生活过得很开心，现在要走了，很舍不得他们，不过以后还有机会，如果有时间，我还会回深圳看看

生词表
INDEX OF VOCABULARY WORDS

A
唉	11
爱好	2
安徽	15
安排	15

B
芭蕾舞	7
把	2
爸爸	14
白兰花	9
半	2
办	12
办法	12
帮	5
榜	10
棒	11
傍晚	1
保持	16
保存	5
保修	5
保养	6
保重	16
宝	9
宝塔	15
报修	5
暴雪	1
暴雨	1
杯	2,10
杯子	14
碑林	15
北方	1
北京	15
本科	13
本来	2
鼻	8
比	1
比邻	16
毕业	13
便利	3
便利店	3
别提了	7
兵马俑	15
冰箱	5
病	8
病毒	8
拨	13
不管……都……	10
不过	1
不好意思	16
不客气	7
不然	11
（不）一样	12
不用	12
不醉不归	10

B
猜	7
猜不着	7
才	4
财政	13
餐馆	3
参加	10
沧浪亭	15
草	9
茶	2
叉	6
差不多	3
产品	6
常	2
常常	1
厂家	5
场	7
场所	10
唱	10
唱歌	10
超市	2
朝	3
潮湿	1
称	9
称……是……	9
成本	4
成份	8
城市	11
吃醋	12
迟到	7
宠物	9
出	5
厨房	3
除了……还……	14
传说	15
吹	6
出口	12
春天	1
从不	1
从来	9
醋	12
存	3,16

D
打	10
打不着	5
打算	7
打针	8
大芬村	14
大理	15
大象	9
大雪	1
大雁塔	15
大雨	1
呆	15

D
代表	10
待遇	13
担心	7
蛋糕	10
当	13
到时	3
倒	12
……的话	12
得	12
登	16
登机	16
等……再……	2
低	1
底	3
地区	1
地址	13
电视	7
电梯	3
电影	7
电子邮件	11
电子邮箱	11
店主	4
丢	5
冬天	4
懂	1
洞庭湖	15
动物	9
动物园	9
堵	5
度	1
短	6
段	16
对不起	5
敦煌	15
多云	1
朵	9
独奏	7
肚子	9
肚子疼	8

E
而且	1
耳朵	9
二胡	2

F
发达	11
发烧	8
发生	12
发现	15
发炎	8
发型	6
繁华	11
犯	8
犯困	8
方便	3

F

防	1
防晒霜	1
房地产	3
房东	3
房（间）	3
房子	3
房主	3
房租	3
放	13
放假	14
放心	16
飞机	12
份	13
风	1
风光	15
风景	11
风土	15
风味	11
幅	14
服用	8
复习	10

G

该……了	5
干	10
干杯	10
干燥	1
感冒	8
感染	8
刚	6
刚才	6
钢琴	2
岗位	13
高	1
高峰	7
高峰期	7
告辞	12
歌	10
歌曲	10
各地	11
各国	11
跟……有关	13
更	6
宫殿	15
公鸡	9
公寓	3
恭喜	12
恭喜发财！	16
工艺品	14
工作经历	13
狗	9
购物	11
古	16
古迹	15
古老	15
顾	12
顾客	6
故事	15
故宫	15
刮	1
怪不得	9
管理	5
管理处	5
光	10
光临	4
广场	11
逛	11
逛街	11
归	10
贵	3
桂林	15
柜子	5
国（家）	9
过	2
过敏	8

H

哈尔滨	1
嗨	11
还好	12
海	16
海岸城	10
害怕	16
航班	12
杭州	15
好喝	9
好玩儿	11
盒	8
合理	10
合同	3
贺卡	10
喉咙疼	8
猴子	9
后来	8
候机室	16
呼伦贝尔大草原	15
胡子	9
户型	3
花	7
画	14
画	14
画画	2
画家	14
话	11
化验	8
化妆品	6
怀念	11
坏	2
欢乐谷	11
环境	10
黄山	15
挥	12
会员	10
或者	14

J

机票	15
继续	13
既……又……	11
加	4
……家	14
家人	14
家电	3
家具	3
假	4
甲	15
假	14
价格	10
间	3
剪	6
剪纸	14
检查	5
简单	13
简历	13
健康状况	13
江苏	15
江西	15
交通	12
脚扭了	8
教育背景	13
教育学	13
接	11
街	11
节	7
结果	8
借光	12
今后	16
金美善	11
锦绣中华	11
近	3
进步	11
精	3
精神	6
经典	10
经济	13
经理	13
经历	13
经验	13
京剧	7
景点	11
九	3
九寨沟	15
酒	10
酒店	15
就要……了	12
旧	4
旧金山	11
焗	6
焗油	6
菊花	9
举	10
句	16
飓风	1
决定	11

K

咖啡	2
开	5,6
开（水）	8
开叉	6
开始	7
开玩笑	9
开心	2
砍价	4
看（望）	14
看报纸	2
看电视	2
看电影	2
看起来	6
康乃馨	9
考试	8
棵	9
咳嗽	8
可	0

K

可爱	9
可口可乐	10
可能	10
课间	10
客厅	3
肯定	4
恐怕	11
孔雀	9
空儿	2
口语	10
夸奖	12
快……了	14
快乐	10
款待	2
……狂	11
昆明	15
困	8

L

啦	4
拉	2
拉肚子	8
拉小提琴	2
蜡烛	10
来不及	12
来得及	7
……来着	10
来自	11
劳驾	12
老虎	9
簕杜鹃	9
雷阵雨	1
离	3
漓江	15
礼物	14
粒	8
厉害	4
历史	11
俩	10
联系	3
脸谱	14
脸型	6
聊天儿	11
陵墓	15
零下	1
另外	3
留	6
留步	2
留园	15
流行	10
柳树	9
楼	3
漏	5
庐山	15
路上	7
录像	7
录用	13
旅客	12
旅游	14

M

嘛	7
马马虎虎	2
马上	5
马桶	5
满意	6
猫	9
玫瑰	7
梅花	9
美发	6
美发店	6
美国	1
美国长岛大学	13
美国长岛大学	13
美容美发厅	6
门锁	5
免费	5
面试官	13
名片	13
名胜	11
明十三陵	15
明天	1
莫高窟	15
茉莉	9
母鸡	9
牡丹	9

N

男	10
难道	12
南方	1
内蒙古	15
能力	13
泥人	14
年轻	11
鸟	9
牛	9
女	10
女孩儿	12
女生	10

O

噢	6
呕吐	8

P

排行	10
排行榜	10
派	5
盘	10
胖	9
泡	9
赔	4
配	12
配套设施	3
喷头	5
朋友	2
批	6
皮肤	6
骗	4
凭	5
平安	16
平（方）米	3
平均	13
平时	10
屏幕	12
鄱阳湖	15
蒲公英	9
普通	6
普通话	11

Q

七夕	7
期	7
期待	13
齐全	3
其实	9
其它	2
骑自行车	2
起来	6
气候	1
气温	1
千	3
签	3
谦虚	2
钱包	14
敲	5
亲爱的	10
秦始皇陵	15
轻	14
清仓	4
清楚	5
青岛	10
晴	1
晴间多云	1
情景	16
情人	6
请教	12
庆祝	10
秋天	1
求职信	13
取	8
取得	13
全	11
却	9

R

染	6
热水器	5
人情	15
人员	3
人质	16
认	12
认识	12
日子	11
榕树	9
如果……就……	10
若	16

S

塞	7
三峡	15
嗓子	8
杀价	4
晒	1
山	15
山东	15
山水	15
善良	12
扇子	14
商量	3
稍微	3
少	1
蛇	9
舍不得	16
身体	9
什么样	11
生病	8
生产	5
生活	16
生气	7
生日	10

S

生意	4	
胜地	15	
胜任	13	
失眠	8	
失望	6	
狮子	9	
狮子林	15	
时	3	
时光	16	
时候	3	
实用	14	
石油	13	
市	9	
是否	13	
事故	12	
世界	11	
世界之窗	11	
收据	5	
收入	13	
手	12	
首	10	
售	5	
舒服	1	
书	14	
输	8	
输液	8	
数	5	
树	9	
甩	4	
甩卖	4	
帅	12	
双	4	
霜	1	
水（江、河、湖、海）	15	
水果	2	
水龙头	5	
水平	2	
睡觉	8	
顺便	6	
顺风	16	
说明	8	
硕士	13	
……死了	4	
寺庙	15	
松树	9	
送	8	
送	14	
送行	16	
苏州	15	
俗语	15	
算	3,12	
算了	4	
算账	12	
虽然……但是……	10	

T

牠们	9
塔	15
台风	1
太湖	15
泰山	15
弹	2

T

弹吉他	2
弹琵琶	2
谈论	1
痰	8
烫	6
掏	7
讨价还价	4
套	3
特别	2
特色	14
疼	8
提	7
提供	13
替	16
天花板	5
天气	1
天堂	15
天下	15
天涯	16
跳舞	2
铁观音	2
听	2
听说	2
听音乐	2
厅	3
通	13
通知	13
同时	10
头	6
头发	6
头晕	8
投资	11
图像	5
兔子	9
团	15
推荐	13

W

玩儿	2
玩电脑	2
玩网络游戏	2
晚	7
晚点	12
晚会	10
万	13
网	11
网上购物	11
网上视频	11
网上下载	11
忘	7
维修	5
为	10
卫生间	3
温	8
文山湖	6
文艺演出	7
闻	9
闻名	14
问候	16
卧室	3
乌龙茶	2
无	12
物	11

X

西安	15

X

西湖	15
西施	6
西药	8
吸引	11
洗发水	6
虾	9
下（面）	3
下（雨）	1
（下）班	7
下雨	1
下水道	5
夏天	1
仙湖植物园	9
羡慕	11
香	9
香槟	10
香港	11
香格里拉	15
想（念）	9
想念	16
享受	10
消炎	8
小时	10
小心	16
小雪	1
小雨	1
效果	6
鞋	4
写作	2
血	8
心	10
心理学	13
心眼儿	12
新加坡	11
辛苦	12
薪金	13
行	4
熊	9
熊猫	9
修	2
修理	2
修理费	5
休息	8
许愿	10
许多	15
……学	13
学历	13
学士	13
学位	13
雪	1

Y

押金	3
鸭子	9
牙疼	8
严重	7
眼（眼睛）	6
眼睛	9
验	8
羊	9
阳（太阳）	3
阳台	3

Y

养	9
样子	6

...Y

药		8
要不		4
要……了		14
钥匙		5
爷爷		14
野餐		1
野生		9
野生动物园		9
液		8
一般		2
一定		10
一共		5
一口价		4
一路		16
一路平安		16
一路顺风		16
一直		15
医生		8
医院		8
遗憾		2
移民		11
颐和园		15
……以内		5
以前		2
以为		4
意思		3
意向		13
音乐		7
音乐会		7
音乐厅		7
阴		1
阴间多云		1
阴天		1
应聘		13
应聘者		13
英文		10
哟		13
优惠		6
油		6
油画		14
邮箱		13
邮政编码		13
有名		14
友谊		10
鱼		9
娱乐		10
雨		1
雨伞		1
预报		1
预约		6
园		9
园林		15
圆		9
原谅		7
岳		15
月亮		10
越来越……		1
乐器		2
云南		15

...Z

再说		12
糟糕		12
早		7
早上		1
赠送		10
张		4,8
张强		13
长		9
账		12
账号		3
账户		3
招聘		13
着		7
找（钱）		4
照		6
照顾		16
珍惜		16
阵		1
阵雨		1
正		6
正常		7
正好		5
只		9
支		10
知己		16
植物		9
植物园		9
值得		15
只好		12
只要……就……		3
至		13
制冷		5
中餐		11
中国		3
中国茶		14
中国工艺品		14
中国画		14
中国结		14
中国书法		14
中介		3
中介人员		3
中雪		1
中雨		1
中药		8
终于		12
猪		9
竹子		9
主管		13
主意		7
祝		10
祝你好运！		16
祝你们白头偕老！早生贵子！		16
祝你圣诞节快乐！		16
祝你生日快乐！		16
祝你心想事成！		16
祝你中秋节快乐！		16
专栏作家		13
专业		5
转行		4
赚		4
装修		3
拙政园		15

...Z

自		11
自己		13
自然		15
自助		15
自助游		15
总（经理）		13
总是		5
走路		3
租		3
租金		3
租客		3
嘴巴		8
醉		10

Discovery Publisher is a multimedia publisher whose mission is to inspire and support personal transformation, spiritual growth and awakening. We strive with every title to preserve the essential wisdom of the author, spiritual teacher, thinker, healer, and visionary artist.

www.ingramcontent.com/pod-product-compliance
Lightning Source LLC
Chambersburg PA
CBHW080516090426

42734CB00015B/3070